60

Miracles

OF

HUMANITY

60 Miracles of Humanity

Rohan Aggarwal

Published by Rohan Aggarwal, 2023.

60 MIRACLES OF HUMANITY

First edition. March 13, 2023.

Copyright © 2023 Rohan Aggarwal.

ISBN: 979-8215215531

Written by Rohan Aggarwal.

Ice, Ice, Baby: The Skating Grandma's Arctic Adventures

Liab is an 80-year-old woman who lives alone in a remote village in Siberia, where everything is frozen. Despite the harsh living conditions, she remains happy and content. She is known as the "Skating Grandma of Siberia" because she often skates on the nearby frozen lake. Liab's story is one of resilience, perseverance, and finding joy in the simplest things.

Liab grew up in Siberia, where the temperature drops rapidly, and the nearby lake freezes for six months every year. As a little girl, she had to skate to go anywhere, and the more she skated, the more she loved it. Skating on the frozen lake became a significant part of her childhood, reminding her of happier, simpler times.

As she grew older, Liab moved away from the lake and the cold weather, finding herself living a normal, boring city life. However, she always took her skates with her wherever she went, which reminded her of the joy she felt when she was a child.

Real life, however, was not as simple as Liab had hoped. She lost her children and husband, leaving her alone and depressed. Liab wanted to go back to a happier time in her life. One day, she packed all her bags and left the city life behind, moving back to her old home in the middle of nowhere.

Despite the harsh living conditions, Liab created a new life for herself. She got herself a small farm and a few animals, which she took care of. She had a lot of work to do, and every day was a new challenge.

She had to dig into the frozen lake to collect water to feed her farm, and sometimes she had to skate for miles and miles to get to nearby towns to buy groceries.

Liab found happiness in the simpler things of life, such as her farm, animals, and her old pair of skates. She started to live a life of simplicity, where she did not need the latest gadgets or the most expensive cars to be happy. Liab's life was not easy, but she found joy in the little things.

Liab's story is an inspiration to many people. She teaches us that we don't need to have everything in life to be happy. Sometimes, the simpler things in life are the ones that bring us the most joy. We often go through life searching for happiness, thinking that we will find it in the biggest houses, the busiest cities, or the latest gadgets. However, Liab's story shows us that happiness is not found in material possessions but in the relationships we build and the simple things we do every day.

Liab's story also teaches us the importance of resilience and perseverance. Despite losing her children and husband, Liab did not give up on life. Instead, she created a new life for herself in the middle of nowhere, where she found joy and contentment in the simplest things.

In conclusion, Liab's story is a reminder that happiness can be found in the simplest things of life. Her resilience, perseverance, and ability to find joy in the little things are inspiring to many. She teaches us that we don't need to have everything in life to be happy and that sometimes the hardest challenges in life can lead to the greatest rewards.

The Class Clown Who Became the World's Best Teacher

Ron Clark is a teacher who believes that education doesn't have to be boring. In fact, he believes that it should be fun and magical, and he has dedicated his career to making that a reality for his students. Clark started his career as a teacher in a low-income area, where he quickly realized that his students were bored and disengaged from traditional textbook learning. In response, he decided to do something different, something that would spark their curiosity and make them excited to learn.

Clark began incorporating music, dance, and theatre into his classroom, creating a lively and engaging environment that his students loved. He even rewrote popular songs to teach his students about history and geography. For example, he changed the lyrics of the Thong Song to teach his students about geography, with lyrics like "Geography is so good to us, we practice and we learn so much, we study that map from front to back, get on the ball now don't be slack, we like to learn about a lot of places that are cool and hot, we study every single spot, from Spain to South Dakota."

Clark's approach worked. His class went from boring to a Broadway show, and his students went from hating school to loving it. Seeing the success he had with his classroom, Clark knew he had to take it to the next level. He decided to build his own school, where learning was magical and students could be engaged in their education like never before.

Clark's school, the Ron Clark Academy, is a unique and inspiring place. Students learn through dance, music, and theatre, and are encouraged to be creative and innovative in their approach to learning. The school has houses like in Harry Potter, and students can hang out with dragons during recess. The school even has slides instead of stairs, which Clark says symbolizes the importance of taking risks and trying new things.

Despite the fun and games, the Ron Clark Academy is also one of the most challenging schools in the world. Students have books and exams and are held to high standards of academic excellence. But because the school is a place of joy and excitement, students are more engaged and motivated to learn. As a result, 95% of the students at the Ron Clark Academy go on to college, with some even making it to Ivy League schools.

Clark believes that every child has the potential to be a future leader, and that it's up to teachers to help them realize that potential. He encourages his staff to look at every student as a future president of the United States, and to prepare them accordingly. He wants his students to be compassionate, knowledgeable, and culturally aware, with an appreciation for other religions and ways of life.

Clark's approach to education is not typical, but it's one that is sorely needed in today's world. With the rise of technology and the constant distractions of modern life, it's more important than ever for teachers to find creative and engaging ways to help their students learn. Clark's success with the Ron Clark Academy shows that it's possible to make education fun and exciting, and that when you do, students are more likely to succeed.

In a world where education is often seen as a chore, Ron Clark is a beacon of hope. He shows us that learning can be an adventure, and that with the right attitude and approach, anything is possible. As we continue to grapple with the challenges of educating young people in the 21st century, we would do well to learn from his example and take a page from his playbook. Education doesn't have to be boring – it can be fun, exciting, and even magical. All we need is a little imagination, creativity, and a lot of heart.

The Garbage Island: Where Sustainability Meets Hospitality

Eric, an environmentalist from Ivory Coast, Africa, decided to take action when he saw how plastic bottles were lining up the beach, poisoning the water, and turning a beautiful coastline into an eyesore. Eric's solution was to collect millions of plastic bottles, tie them together, and create a floating hotel that is now a successful business attracting over 100 visitors per week.

Eric's floating hotel is not only a unique business but is also an eco-friendly solution to the problem of plastic waste. The hotel has its own solar panels for energy and equipment to turn waste into fertilizer. The hotel's existence is a testament to the potential of using waste products in innovative ways.

Eric's floating hotel is a product of his passion for the environment. He was obsessed with trash and believed that nothing goes to waste. Eric's solution to the plastic waste problem is inspiring because it shows that no idea is too crazy to make a difference. He is determined to change the way people look at trash and find a different use for it.

Eric's solution to the plastic waste problem is also an example of how individuals can make a difference in their communities. Eric saw a problem and decided to take action, inspiring his country to follow his lead. He is planning to get more plastics and build even more islands and get the whole Ivory Coast to help so that one day the coastline of this beautiful country will be plastic-free.

Eric's solution to the plastic waste problem is an excellent example of how technology can be used to address environmental issues. The floating hotel is an innovative solution that uses waste products in a way that benefits both the environment and the economy. Eric's hotel shows that technology can be used for sustainable development, promoting economic growth while also addressing environmental challenges.

Eric's floating hotel is an example of how innovation can be used to address environmental challenges. Eric's idea was crazy, but he saw an opportunity to create something new out of waste. Eric's hotel shows that innovation can be a powerful tool for addressing environmental problems.

Eric's floating hotel is an example of how businesses can be sustainable and profitable. Eric's hotel is a successful business that attracts over 100 visitors per week. The hotel's success is a testament to the potential of businesses that are both environmentally conscious and profitable.

Eric's floating hotel is an example of how education can be used to address environmental problems. Eric is teaching children about the importance of not throwing trash in nature. Eric's efforts to educate children about the environment will ensure that future generations will be more environmentally conscious.

Eric's floating hotel is an example of how collaboration can be used to address environmental problems. Eric is getting the whole Ivory Coast to help so that one day the coastline of this beautiful country will be plastic-free. Eric's efforts show that collaboration is key to addressing environmental challenges.

Eric's floating hotel is an example of how individuals can inspire their communities to take action. Eric's hotel has inspired Ivory Coast to take action against plastic waste. Eric's efforts show that individuals can be powerful agents of change in their communities.

In conclusion, Eric's floating hotel is an inspiring solution to the plastic waste problem. Eric saw a problem and decided to take action, inspiring his country to follow his lead. Eric's hotel is a unique and eco-friendly business that shows the potential of using waste products in innovative ways. Eric's hotel is an example of how technology, innovation, education, collaboration, and individual action can be used to address environmental challenges. Eric's hotel shows that no idea is too crazy to make a difference.

The Swiss Isolation Experiment: One Man's Quest for Happiness

Xavier's story is one of the unique ways that people have attempted to find happiness and meaning in their lives. His journey of leaving his life in Switzerland behind to live on an isolated island for 300 days may seem extreme, but it highlights the importance of finding what brings joy and fulfilment to one's life, even if it means going against societal norms.

In today's world, it is easy to get caught up in the hustle and bustle of daily life. Many people fall into a pattern of working a nine-to-five job, buying a house, and acquiring material possessions to find happiness. However, these things do not always bring lasting happiness, and many people find themselves feeling unfulfilled and unhappy.

Xavier's decision to leave behind the trappings of modern life and immerse himself in nature shows the importance of connecting with the world around us. By living in isolation, Xavier was forced to rely on his own abilities to survive, and he found joy in the smallest things, such as building a bench or growing a garden. This highlights the fact that material possessions and wealth are not necessary for happiness, and true joy can come from living a simple, meaningful life.

However, it is also important to note that Xavier's journey was not without its challenges. He faced the physical and mental challenges of living in isolation, dealing with loneliness and boredom, and learning how to survive in the wild. This shows that finding happiness and meaning in life is not always easy, and it may require taking risks and facing difficulties.

While not everyone may be able to or willing to embark on a journey like Xavier's, there are still ways to find happiness and meaning in life. One way is to focus on personal growth and development. This can include pursuing hobbies, learning new skills, and challenging oneself to step out of their comfort zone. By pushing oneself to grow and improve, individuals can find a sense of purpose and fulfilment that goes beyond material possessions or societal expectations.

Another way to find happiness is to connect with others. Building relationships with family, friends, and the wider community can provide a sense of belonging and purpose. Engaging in acts of kindness and service can also be a source of happiness, as it allows individuals to make a positive impact on others.

In addition, connecting with nature can be a powerful way to find peace and happiness. Spending time in nature has been shown to reduce stress and anxiety, boost mood, and promote physical and mental health. This can include activities such as hiking, camping, or simply spending time in a park or garden.

Ultimately, the key to finding happiness and meaning in life is to focus on what brings joy and fulfilment, rather than simply following societal norms or chasing material possessions. This may require taking risks and facing challenges, but the rewards can be immense.

In conclusion, Xavier's journey of living alone on an island for 300 days highlights the importance of finding what brings joy and meaning to one's life, even if it means going against societal norms. While not everyone may be able or willing to embark on such a journey, there are still ways to find happiness and fulfilment, such as focusing on personal growth, connecting with others, and connecting with nature. By prioritizing what brings joy and meaning, individuals can find lasting happiness and fulfilment in their lives.

Breaking Records and Stereotypes: The Girl Who Shook Up F1 Racing

The world of Formula One (F1) racing has long been dominated by men. There has never been a female driver who has won an F1 race. However, this may soon change with the emergence of young female racers like Juju, who aspires to be the first female driver to win an F1 race. Juju's story is an inspiration to many young girls who dream of entering the male-dominated world of motorsports.

Juju's passion for racing started at a young age. Growing up in Japan, she was fascinated with cars and speed. While most girls her age were playing with dolls, Juju was playing with cars. She learned to race as soon as she learned to talk. Her father recognized her passion and supported her dream of becoming a professional racer.

Juju's first foray into racing was in cart races. She won her first race and continued to win race after race. Her father believed that she was ready for bigger races, such as F1. He believed that his daughter could compete with the best drivers in the world, regardless of gender.

However, not everyone shared Juju's father's optimism. There are many people who believe that women are not as skilled as men in racing. They argue that the physical demands of racing require greater strength and endurance, which men have an advantage over women. However, these beliefs are being challenged by young female racers like Juju.

In recent years, more and more women have been entering the world of motorsports. They are proving that they can compete with the best drivers in the world. In 2020, the W Series was created, a racing series exclusively for women. The W Series aims to provide female racers with the opportunity to compete at a high level and prove that they can be just as skilled as their male counterparts.

Juju's story is an example of the importance of parental support in achieving one's dreams. Her father believed in her abilities and provided her with the resources and opportunities to pursue her passion. He did not let gender stereotypes or societal expectations hold his daughter back. He saw the potential in his daughter and supported her every step of the way.

The lack of representation of women in motorsports is not unique to F1. It is a problem that plagues many other sports as well. There are still many people who believe that certain sports are not suited for women, whether it is due to physical differences or cultural norms. However, this mindset is slowly changing, thanks to the efforts of female athletes and their supporters.

It is important to provide young girls with role models and opportunities to pursue their passions, regardless of gender. By doing so, we can break down gender stereotypes and empower the next generation of female athletes. It is also important to challenge the status quo and push for greater representation of women in male-dominated fields.

In conclusion, Juju's story is a testament to the power of determination and the importance of parental support. She is breaking down barriers and proving that women can compete with the best in the world of motorsports. Her story is an inspiration to many young girls who dream of entering the male-dominated world of F1 racing. We must continue to support and encourage female athletes, challenge gender stereotypes, and push for greater representation of women in all fields.

Hair Raising Tales from the Village of Long Locks

The Village of Long Hair Women is an example of how culture and tradition can shape people's values and beliefs. Located in a small village a thousand miles from Beijing, this community of women has been growing their hair for hundreds of years, creating a unique identity for themselves that has caught the attention of the world.

The women of the village see their hair as more than just a physical feature, but rather as a link to their ancestors and a symbol of their cultural heritage. Hair is an integral part of their identity, and the tradition of growing long hair has been passed down from generation to generation. As such, hair care is taken very seriously, with hours dedicated to combing and washing their hair to keep it healthy and beautiful.

One of the reasons why the women in the village are so famous is because they have managed to grow their hair to extreme lengths, with some women's hair reaching 1.5 meters long and weighing as much as one kilogram. This is a remarkable feat, considering that hair usually grows at a rate of about 0.5 inches per month, which means that it would take years to grow hair that long.

To maintain the quality and beauty of their hair, the women in the village use a special homemade shampoo made from rice water, herbs, fruits, and tea. This shampoo is an essential part of their hair care routine, and it is used regularly to keep their hair healthy and shiny.

Another interesting aspect of the tradition of long hair in the village is the fact that the women only cut their hair once in their entire lives, on their 17th birthday night. This is a significant event, and it is celebrated with great pomp and ceremony. The cutting of the hair symbolizes a rite of passage from childhood to adulthood, and it is a way for the women to connect with their cultural heritage.

Over the years, the village has become famous, and tourists from all over the world travel there to admire the beauty of the women's hair and to learn about their hair care secrets. The women are happy to share their knowledge and their homemade shampoo recipe, which is given out for free to anyone who is interested.

The story of the Village of Long Hair Women is a fascinating example of how culture and tradition can shape people's values and beliefs. The women in the village have managed to maintain a tradition that has been passed down from generation to generation, and they have turned it into a source of pride and identity.

The story also highlights the importance of cultural preservation and the need to respect and value different cultural practices. In a world where globalization and cultural homogenization are becoming increasingly common, it is important to recognize and appreciate the diversity of cultures that exist around the world.

In conclusion, the Village of Long Hair Women is a unique example of how a simple tradition can become a source of identity and pride for an entire community. The women in the village have managed to maintain a tradition that has been passed down from generation to generation, and they have turned it into a source of beauty and admiration. Their story serves as a reminder of the importance of cultural preservation and the need to respect and value different cultural practices.

The Educator Carpenter: Meet America's Zooming Hero

Nate Evans, an elementary school teacher from Iowa, has become known as America's Best Zoom Teacher due to his efforts to build desks for his students during the pandemic. The COVID-19 pandemic has caused schools across the United States to switch to remote learning, leaving many students without a proper workspace at home. Evans recognized this problem and decided to take matters into his own hands.

Evans' story began in early 2020, when schools in Iowa closed due to the pandemic. He noticed that many of his students were taking notes from the floor, kitchen table, or their beds, and realized that they could benefit from having a dedicated workspace. He believed that having a designated space to study would help his students focus and learn better, but many of them did not have access to a desk at home.

Evans decided to use his woodworking skills to build desks for his students. He had started his own woodworking company four years earlier, and felt that he could put his skills to use for a good cause. He began building basic desks after school hours, using his own money to purchase the materials. Each desk cost him $30 to make and took about an hour to build. He would then spend another hour and a half delivering the desks to his students in his minivan.

Initially, Evans planned to build just a few desks for his students. However, as word spread about his efforts, more and more people became interested in helping out. Evans received donations from local businesses and individuals, and volunteers came forward to assist with the building and delivery of the desks. He also started a GoFundMe page to raise funds for the project.

Despite facing several challenges, including a diagnosis of a tumour in his arm, Evans continued building desks for his students. He believed that a simple desk could make a big difference in a child's education, and he was determined to help as many students as possible. He even went above and beyond, building specialized desks for students with disabilities and creating desks with storage space for school supplies.

Evans' efforts have been incredibly impactful. His dedication and hard work have helped many students have a dedicated space to study at home. The desks have not only improved their learning experience, but have also given them a sense of ownership and responsibility over their own education. As one mother put it, the desks have made their lives much more organized, and each child now has their own space to grow and learn.

Evans' story is a testament to the power of individual action and community support. He saw a problem in his own community and took it upon himself to find a solution. His efforts inspired others to get involved, and together they were able to make a significant difference in the lives of many students. In a time of great uncertainty and challenges, Evans' story serves as a reminder that we can all do our part to make a positive impact on those around us.

The Zen of Youth: A Child's Path to Inner Peace and Enlightenment

Tobey, the 15-year-old yoga teacher from California, has become a sensation as the youngest yoga guru in the world. His story is remarkable not just for his young age but also for the dedication and selflessness he has shown in his pursuit of healing and helping others.

Tobey's journey began when he was just six years old, and his mother was diagnosed with cancer. After a long and difficult battle with drugs and chemotherapy, Tobey's mother discovered the healing power of yoga, and within a few months of practicing yoga, she was able to walk on her own and was happier and healthier than before. Tobey saw first-hand how yoga had transformed his mother's life, and he became inspired to become a yoga teacher and help others experience the same transformation.

What sets Tobey apart is not just his age but also his unwavering commitment to his mission. When he expressed his desire to become a yoga teacher at the age of six, many assumed it was just a passing phase. However, Tobey was determined to pursue his goal, and he quit meat, learned about nutrition, turned vegan, and started training to become a yoga teacher. His dedication paid off when he became the youngest yoga teacher in the US.

But Tobey's achievements go beyond just his status as a yoga teacher. He is also a genius who doubled up on his high school classes and graduated at the age of 14, a remarkable feat that is even more impressive considering his other commitments as a yoga teacher.

What makes Tobey a remarkable yoga teacher is not just his technical expertise but also his approach to teaching. He approaches his students with love and provides emotional healing through his classes, creating a safe and nurturing space where his students can connect with their bodies and find inner peace. His students, some as old as 89, leave his classes in awe of what a great teacher and what a great experience they have had.

But Tobey's achievements do not end there. He donates most of the money he earns to cancer patients who he teaches yoga and nutrition for free. Despite his young age, Tobey has already made a significant impact on the lives of those he has helped, and his selfless approach to teaching and giving back is an inspiration to others.

Tobey's story is a powerful reminder that age is just a number and that it is never too early or too late to pursue your dreams and make a difference in the world. His dedication, commitment, and selflessness are a testament to the power of yoga and the impact that one individual can have when they follow their passion and purpose.

In a world that is often focused on material success and personal gain, Tobey's story is a refreshing reminder of the importance of giving back and helping others. His example shows that even at a young age, it is possible to make a significant impact on the world and that true success lies not in what we achieve for ourselves but in how we help others.

In conclusion, Tobey's story is an inspiring reminder that age is just a number, and it is never too early or too late to pursue our dreams and make a difference in the world. Tobey's unwavering dedication, commitment, and selflessness in pursuing his mission to help others through yoga and nutrition are an inspiration to all of us. His story shows that we can all make a difference in the world, no matter our age or circumstances, and that true success lies in how we help others.

The Ultimate Disguise: How She Fooled Everyone

The story of Sisa is a fascinating one, highlighting the difficult situations many women face around the world. Living in a society where women were expected to stay at home and raise children, Sisa found herself abandoned and without the financial means to provide for her daughter. In response, she made the decision to live as a man, taking on jobs that were reserved for men in her society, such as construction work and shining shoes.

Sisa's story is not unique. Women around the world face similar challenges, where societal expectations and norms limit their opportunities and leave them vulnerable. This is especially true in developing countries where poverty and lack of education further exacerbate the problem. Women are often relegated to domestic roles, and their voices are silenced in matters of politics and decision-making.

In many cases, women like Sisa find themselves forced to take drastic measures in order to survive. They may resort to living as men or even selling their bodies for money. These actions are not choices made out of desire but rather out of necessity. It is a tragedy that women have to sacrifice their identity and dignity in order to provide for themselves and their families.

Sisa's decision to live as a man was not an easy one. She faced discrimination and isolation from her own family and community. But she persevered and became stronger, both physically and mentally.

Sisa's story is a testament to the resilience of women and their ability to adapt to difficult circumstances.

However, Sisa's story also highlights the fact that women who take such drastic measures often forget how to be a woman. They lose touch with their femininity and their identity, and this can have long-lasting effects on their mental and emotional health. The pressure to conform to societal expectations can be suffocating, leaving women feeling trapped and helpless.

It is important to note that while Sisa's story has a happy ending, millions of women around the world continue to suffer in silence. They are denied education, healthcare, and political representation. They are subject to violence and discrimination, and their voices are not heard.

To address this problem, governments and societies must take action to ensure that women are given equal opportunities and rights. This includes improving access to education and healthcare, promoting gender equality, and enforcing laws that protect women's rights. Women must be given the freedom to make their own choices and pursue their own dreams, without fear of judgment or discrimination.

It is also important for men to take an active role in promoting gender equality. Men must recognize their privilege and work towards creating a more equitable society. This includes supporting women's education and employment, promoting women's political representation, and speaking out against violence and discrimination.

In conclusion, Sisa's story is a powerful reminder of the challenges faced by women around the world. It highlights the need for society to take action to promote gender equality and provide opportunities for women to thrive. Women must be given the freedom to make their own choices and pursue their own dreams, without fear of judgment or discrimination. Men must also take an active role in promoting gender equality and working towards a more equitable society. Only by working together can we create a world where all women are able to live their lives to the fullest.

Ass-isting Education: Donkeys and Their Saddlebags of Books

In many parts of the world, access to books and education is not a given. Children who grow up in poverty often do not have access to educational resources, including books, which can limit their opportunities and impact their ability to succeed in life. This is a significant challenge in developing countries where access to education is limited, and people live in remote areas far away from libraries and schools.

Luis Soriano, a village teacher in Colombia, recognized this problem and decided to do something about it. He noticed that many children in his community were growing up without reading books, which he believed was hindering their education and their futures. To address this issue, he created a mobile library, which he carried on the backs of two donkeys, Alpha and Beta.

Luis travelled to remote areas on the backs of his donkeys, bringing books to children who had limited access to educational resources. He believed that the books he carried could change the lives of these children and help them succeed in life. Luis's mobile library became a lifeline for many children who were hungry for knowledge and thirsty for education.

Luis's dedication and commitment to education did not waver, even when faced with adversity. He continued to travel on the backs of his donkeys, even after he lost his legs. He did not ask for anything in return, and his selflessness and dedication to education became an inspiration to many people in Colombia and around the world.

Luis's story highlights the importance of education and the challenges that many people face in accessing it. In many parts of the world, access to education is limited, and children grow up without basic literacy skills. This not only limits their opportunities but also contributes to a cycle of poverty and lack of social mobility.

Access to education is a critical issue that needs to be addressed on a global scale. Providing access to books, libraries, and educational resources is essential to breaking the cycle of poverty and promoting social mobility. Organizations and individuals like Luis Soriano are playing a crucial role in providing access to education in places where it is limited.

Advancements in technology have made it possible to provide educational resources to people who live in remote areas. The Internet has made it possible for people to access educational resources online, regardless of where they live. However, even with these advancements, access to education remains limited in many parts of the world.

AI has the potential to play a significant role in providing access to education in remote areas. AI-powered educational tools can help people learn and access educational resources online. AI-powered chatbots, for example, can answer questions and provide guidance to students who are studying remotely. AI-powered tutors can provide personalized feedback and support to students who need it, regardless of where they live.

AI can also be used to improve the quality of education. AI-powered tools can analyse data and identify areas where students are struggling. This information can be used to create personalized learning plans that address individual student needs. AI-powered educational games and simulations can make learning more engaging and interactive, improving student outcomes.

While AI has the potential to improve access to education and promote social mobility, it is not a silver bullet. Access to education is a complex issue that requires a multi-faceted approach. Governments, NGOs, and private organizations must work together to provide access to educational resources in remote areas. AI can play a role in this effort, but it must be part of a broader strategy that addresses the root causes of limited access to education.

In conclusion, Luis Soriano's story is a testament to the power of education and the impact that individuals can make when they are committed to a cause. His mobile library on the backs of two donkeys brought knowledge and education to children who had limited access to resources. Access to education remains a critical issue in many parts of the world, and AI has the potential.

Inked and Aged: World's Oldest Tattoo Artist Still Going Strong

Tattooing is an ancient form of body art that has been around for thousands of years. It has been practiced in various cultures across the world, with different meanings and purposes. In the Philippines, tattooing has a rich history that dates back to pre-colonial times. Tattooing was once a sacred ritual in the Philippines, and tattoos were seen as symbols of bravery, strength, and identity. They were used to mark important life events such as birth, death, marriage, and war. However, over time, the tradition of tattooing faded away, and it is now only practiced by a few people.

One of the last remaining tattoo artists in the Philippines is Whang-Od, a 103-year-old woman who lives in a remote village in the mountains of Kalinga, in the northern part of the country. Whang-Od is not just a tattoo artist, but a living legend, a master of a fading art, and a cultural icon. She is the oldest and the most famous traditional tattoo artist in the Philippines and is often referred to as the "last mambabatok" or the last traditional Kalinga tattooist. Her skill and artistry have attracted tattoo enthusiasts and anthropologists from around the world, who come to her village to witness and experience the ancient art of Kalinga tattooing.

Whang-Od's tattoos are not just body art but are cultural artifacts that reflect the Kalinga's history, beliefs, and way of life. Her tattoos are made up of a combination of geometric patterns, symbols, and animal motifs that represent the wearer's status, achievements, and character.

For example, a tattoo of a centipede is believed to bring good luck, while a tattoo of a scorpion is meant to protect the wearer from evil spirits. A tattoo of a ladder symbolizes the wearer's ambition and desire to climb the social ladder.

Whang-Od's tattoos are not only unique and meaningful but are also made using traditional tools and methods. Unlike modern tattoo machines that use electric needles to inject ink into the skin, Whang-Od uses a traditional "thorn" or "bamboo" needle, which is made by attaching a thorn or bamboo stick to the end of a wooden handle. The needle is dipped into a mixture of soot and water, which is then tapped into the skin using a stick. This process is not only painful but also time-consuming and requires a great deal of skill and precision.

Whang-Od's tattoos are not just a reflection of the Kalinga culture but are also a link to a lost history. The Kalinga tattoos were once used to mark warriors, who would wear them as symbols of their bravery and achievements. The tattoos were also used to protect the wearer from harm during battle. The tradition of Kalinga tattooing was once widespread in the region, with many tattoo artists practicing the art. However, with the advent of modernization and the decline of the Kalinga culture, the tradition of tattooing slowly faded away, and Whang-Od became one of the last remaining practitioners of the art.

Whang-Od's story is a testament to the resilience and adaptability of traditional cultures in the face of modernization. She has not only preserved the ancient art of Kalinga tattooing but has also adapted it to meet the demands of the modern world. While traditional Kalinga tattoos were once reserved for warriors and members of the community, Whang-Od now tattoos tourists who come from all over the world to experience the ancient art form.

Whang-Od's tattoos have become so popular that they have become a tourist attraction in their own right. Visitors to her village not only get a chance to get a tattoo from the last traditional Kalinga tattoo artist but also get to experience the rich culture and heritage of the Kalinga people. The tattoos have become a way for visitors to connect with the Kalinga culture and to keep the tradition alive.

Whang-Od's story is a reminder that traditional cultures and practices are not static but are constantly evolving and adapting to changing circumstances. While modernization and globalization have led to the decline of many traditional practices, there are still those who are determined to preserve and promote their heritage. Whang-Od's tattoos are not just a form of body art but are also a symbol of resilience and cultural pride. Her story is an inspiration to all those who are fighting to preserve their culture and heritage in the face of modernization.

The Human Hard Drive: A Comical Take on a Man with Perfect Recall

Memory is a fundamental aspect of human experience. Memories allow us to learn, grow, and reflect on our past experiences. For most people, however, memory is not a perfect record of their lives. It is common for memories to fade or become distorted over time, making it difficult to recall specific details about past events accurately. However, some individuals possess exceptional memories that enable them to recall vivid and detailed information about events in their lives.

Bob Petrella is one such person. His memory is so exceptional that he can recall details about events from his life with remarkable precision. He can remember the date, time, weather, and other specific details of events that occurred years ago. Bob was unaware of his unique ability until his friends asked him about a birthday party he attended ten years before, and he was able to describe the entire event in detail. His friends were amazed, and they began to ask him about other events, which Bob also recalled with great accuracy.

Bob's extraordinary memory has been studied by doctors for over 20 years, but they still do not fully understand how he is able to remember so much. Some researchers believe that his brain has a more extensive network of connections that allows him to retrieve memories more efficiently. Others suggest that his exceptional memory is due to his ability to create associations between different pieces of information, which makes it easier for him to retrieve them later.

While having a strong memory may seem like a superpower, it also comes with challenges. Bob has difficulty forgetting negative experiences, which can lead to anxiety and depression. For example, when his brother passed away, Bob had to battle with intense grief and found it challenging to move on. He also struggles with reliving unpleasant experiences, such as breakups or conflicts, with greater intensity than most people. He has learned to manage his emotions by focusing on positive memories and using them to help him through difficult times.

Bob's story highlights the complexity of memory and the challenges that come with having an exceptional memory. While many people struggle to remember important details about their lives, Bob's ability to recall events with such precision is a reminder of the vast range of human experience. It also raises important questions about how memory works and what factors contribute to individual differences in memory abilities.

Research on exceptional memory is still in its early stages, but it holds promise for understanding how the brain stores and retrieves memories. It may also have implications for treating memory-related disorders, such as Alzheimer's disease, and for developing new memory-enhancing techniques.

In conclusion, Bob Petrella's exceptional memory is a fascinating example of the diversity of human experience. While his ability to remember events with such precision is rare, it also comes with challenges, such as difficulty forgetting negative experiences. His story highlights the complexity of memory and the many factors that contribute to individual differences in memory abilities. As research in this area continues to advance, we may gain a better understanding of how memory works and how we can enhance our ability to remember important details about our lives.

The Moist Messiah of Kenya's Creatures

Patrick Kilonzo Mwalua, also known as the Crazy Water King of Kenya, has been capturing the world's attention since 2016 for his selfless act of delivering water to wild animals in Tsavo West National Park, Kenya, during the drought season. In the past, the park was covered with waterholes that the animals relied on for their daily needs, but with the impacts of climate change, the region has experienced a significant decrease in rainfall, resulting in the drying up of many water sources. As a result, the animals were forced to travel for long distances to find water, making it difficult for them to survive.

Patrick, who grew up in a family of farmers in Kenya, began to notice the devastating effects of climate change on the wildlife in his area. Determined to make a difference, Patrick decided to take action and started delivering water to the park using his personal truck. He would fill up his truck with fresh water from a nearby town and drive it to the park, traveling over 70 miles each day.

Despite being warned of the risks of approaching wild animals, Patrick persisted in his mission to save them from dying of thirst. His bravery and selflessness have earned him recognition worldwide, and his work has inspired many people to take action against climate change.

Patrick's actions highlight the importance of protecting and preserving our environment. Climate change is causing unprecedented harm to our planet, from devastating natural disasters to the loss of entire species. As the world's population continues to grow, we must take urgent action to protect our planet and its inhabitants.

One of the most significant challenges in addressing climate change is the need for international cooperation. Climate change is a global problem that requires a global solution. International agreements such as the Paris Agreement are essential in addressing climate change as they provide a framework for countries to work together to reduce greenhouse gas emissions and limit the global temperature increase.

Another critical factor in addressing climate change is individual action. While international cooperation is crucial, it is also vital for individuals to take action in their daily lives. This includes reducing our carbon footprint by using public transport or biking, using renewable energy sources, and reducing our consumption of animal products. By taking small steps in our daily lives, we can collectively make a significant impact in reducing greenhouse gas emissions and limiting the impacts of climate change.

Patrick's work is also an example of the importance of community involvement in environmental conservation. By involving local communities in conservation efforts, we can help to ensure that conservation efforts are sustainable and that they benefit both the environment and local communities. Local communities are often the most affected by climate change, and their participation is essential in developing effective solutions.

In conclusion, Patrick Kilonzo Mwalua's work as the Crazy Water King of Kenya is a testament to the power of individual action in addressing climate change. His selflessness, bravery, and dedication have inspired many people worldwide to take action against climate change. However, Patrick's work is not enough to solve the global problem of climate change. We need to take urgent action at all levels, from individual action to international cooperation, to address this global crisis. By working together, we can protect our planet and ensure a sustainable future for generations to come.

The Vault for Those Who Were Told They Never Would

Chetna Gala Sinha, a social activist and entrepreneur, founded the Mann Deshi Mahila Sahakari Bank in 1997. This bank is exclusively for poor women in rural areas of India who do not have access to formal banking services. The bank provides a wide range of services to women, including savings accounts, loans, insurance, and financial literacy training. The bank also encourages entrepreneurship among its customers by providing small business loans and training programs.

Chetna Gala Sinha's inspiration for starting the bank came from her own experiences as a young woman in Mumbai. She saw first-hand how women from low-income backgrounds were denied access to financial services because of their lack of education and social status. She realized that providing these women with access to banking services would not only help them financially, but would also empower them and help them break out of the cycle of poverty.

However, starting a bank for poor women was not an easy task. Chetna Gala Sinha faced numerous challenges, including obtaining a banking license, training women who had little to no formal education, and convincing people that poor women were creditworthy. To overcome these challenges, she mobilized a team of local women and started teaching them about banking and finance. She also leveraged her network of contacts to secure funding and support for the bank.

The bank has been incredibly successful, and today it has more than 170,000 account holders and has loaned over 50 million dollars. It has also inspired other banks and financial institutions to start similar initiatives to provide financial services to the poor. The Mann Deshi Mahila Sahakari Bank has become a model for how to provide financial services to marginalized communities in a sustainable and socially responsible manner.

One of the unique features of the bank is its focus on financial literacy. The bank runs regular training programs for its customers to help them understand financial concepts and manage their finances more effectively. This has helped women to not only save money but also to invest in businesses and generate income. By providing women with access to financial services and the knowledge to use them effectively, the bank has helped to empower them and improve their standard of living.

Another key feature of the bank is its focus on entrepreneurship. The bank provides small business loans to women who want to start their own businesses. It also provides training programs on business management, marketing, and financial planning. By providing women with the resources and knowledge they need to start and grow their own businesses, the bank has helped to create a culture of entrepreneurship and self-reliance among its customers.

The Mann Deshi Mahila Sahakari Bank has also been a pioneer in using technology to provide financial services to its customers. The bank was one of the first in India to introduce mobile banking services, which allows customers to access their accounts and make transactions using their mobile phones. The bank has also experimented with using biometric authentication to provide secure access to accounts without the need for PINs or passwords. By using technology to make banking more accessible and convenient, the bank has been able to reach more customers and provide better services.

In conclusion, the Mann Deshi Mahila Sahakari Bank is an inspiring example of how social entrepreneurship can be used to address social and economic problems in a sustainable and impactful way. Chetna Gala Sinha's vision and determination have created a bank that has helped to empower thousands of women in rural India and has become a model for other financial institutions around the world. The bank's focus on financial literacy, entrepreneurship, and technology has helped to create a more inclusive and equitable financial system, and its success shows that providing financial services to marginalized communities is not only a moral imperative but also a smart business decision.

Om and Drop the Bass: The Beatboxing Monk Who Found Nirvana

Yukitsu, the Japanese monk who beatboxes and teaches religion on YouTube, is a unique example of how one can find meaning in unexpected places. His story highlights the power of following one's passions and finding ways to incorporate them into one's work, even if that work is traditionally seen as serious or sombre.

Yukitsu's journey to becoming a monk was not a straight path. He started as a musician, playing for almost twenty years before deciding to make a drastic change in his life. Six years ago, he chose to become a monk, drawn to the meaning he found in religion. However, he did not give up music completely. He continued to play music at night, even after spending his days performing funerals and religious services.

It was during this time that Yukitsu discovered his talent for beatboxing. He realized that he could mix his passion for music with his newfound vocation as a monk. The combination of the two seemed strange, and it was certainly different from the traditional image of a monk. However, Yukitsu's unique approach to teaching religion through beatboxing worked, and he gained a large following on YouTube.

Yukitsu's approach to teaching religion through beatboxing might seem unorthodox, but it is not without precedent. Buddhism has a long tradition of incorporating music into religious practice. In fact, chanting and singing are integral parts of Buddhist ceremonies, and the use of music and other sensory experiences can be powerful tools for achieving a meditative state.

Yukitsu's use of beatboxing in religious practice can be seen as an extension of this tradition. Beatboxing is a form of vocal percussion that involves creating rhythm and sounds using only one's mouth. It is a unique art form that requires both technical skill and creativity. Yukitsu's beatboxing is particularly impressive because he is able to integrate it with Buddhist chants, creating a hybrid of traditional and modern forms of expression.

Yukitsu's popularity on YouTube is a testament to the power of social media to connect people across cultures and language barriers. His beatboxing videos have reached millions of viewers around the world, and his unique approach to teaching religion has resonated with people of all backgrounds. This highlights the potential of social media platforms to facilitate cultural exchange and understanding.

Furthermore, Yukitsu's story highlights the importance of finding meaning in one's work. He was able to find a way to incorporate his passion for music into his religious practice, creating a unique approach to teaching that has gained a large following. This is a reminder that work can be more than just a means of making a living; it can also be a source of personal fulfillment and growth.

In conclusion, Yukitsu's story is a unique example of how one can find meaning in unexpected places. His journey from musician to monk to beatboxing teacher highlights the importance of following one's passions and finding ways to incorporate them into one's work. His use of beatboxing in religious practice can be seen as an extension of the Buddhist tradition of using music to achieve a meditative state. Finally, his popularity on YouTube demonstrates the power of social media to facilitate cultural exchange and understanding.

What do you get when you adopt 80 kids? A lifetime supply of Father's Day cards

The story of Mohammad Bzeek is a heart-warming and inspiring one, as he has dedicated his life to caring for children with terminal illnesses who have been abandoned by their families. He has adopted over 80 such children, providing them with the love, care, and support they need to live out their last days with dignity and joy.

Born and raised in Libya, Mohammad moved to the United States decades ago in search of a better life. However, instead of finding the American dream, he discovered a heart-breaking reality - children with terminal illnesses who were abandoned by their families and left to die alone in hospitals. These children had no one to care for them, no one to love them, and no one to provide for them.

Mohammad knew he had to do something about this. He could not stand by and watch these children die alone, without a family or anyone to comfort them. So he decided to bring them home and adopt them as his own children.

It is difficult to imagine the pain and suffering these children must have gone through, and the sense of abandonment and isolation they must have felt. But for Mohammad, every child deserves to have a family and a home, even if it is only for a short time. He believes that every child has a right to be loved and cared for, and that no child should ever have to die alone.

Mohammad's story is a powerful reminder of the importance of compassion and empathy in our world today. It is easy to become numb to the suffering of others, especially when it is so overwhelming and seemingly insurmountable. But Mohammad shows us that even one person can make a difference, that even one person can bring light and love into the lives of those who are suffering.

His story also reminds us of the many challenges that caregivers of children with terminal illnesses face. These children require a tremendous amount of care and attention, as well as expensive treatments and medications. It is a testament to Mohammad's strength and determination that he has been able to provide for so many children, even in the face of his own health struggles.

In addition, Mohammad's story raises important questions about the role of society in caring for the most vulnerable among us. Why are there so many children with terminal illnesses who are abandoned by their families? Why are there not more resources and support systems in place to care for these children? What can we do as a society to ensure that every child, regardless of their health or circumstances, has a family and a home?

These questions are not easy to answer, but they are essential if we are to build a more compassionate and just society. Mohammad's story reminds us that we all have a responsibility to care for one another, especially those who are most in need.

In conclusion, Mohammad Bzeek's story is a powerful testament to the strength of the human spirit and the power of compassion and empathy. He has shown us that even in the face of overwhelming suffering and heartbreak, it is possible to bring light and love into the lives of those who are suffering. His story is a call to action, a reminder that we all have a responsibility to care for one another, especially those who are most vulnerable.

How to Tile Your Way to a Greener Future with Carbon

Tejas Sidnal's innovation of turning carbon waste into tiles is a significant breakthrough in the field of sustainable construction. As the world population grows, so does the demand for modern infrastructure and architecture, leading to increased pollution levels. The construction industry is responsible for a considerable amount of carbon emissions, which has become a significant contributor to global warming and climate change. The need for sustainable building materials and practices is now more critical than ever.

Carbon waste is one of the major by-products of industrial processes, particularly in the production of tires and other rubber products. These waste materials are usually burnt off, releasing tons of carbon dioxide into the atmosphere, contributing to air pollution. Tejas Sidnal's idea of using this carbon waste to make tiles is a sustainable solution that not only reduces pollution but also creates a value-added product.

The process of turning carbon waste into tiles is complex and involves several steps. Firstly, the carbon waste is collected from factories, and then it is processed in a lab to remove impurities and contaminants. Then, the purified carbon waste is mixed with other materials to make it stronger and more durable. The resulting material is sent to artisan factories where it is molded into tiles by hand. The final product is unique and has a distinctive design, making it an attractive option for architects and designers.

One of the significant advantages of these tiles is their environmental impact. They come with zero waste and zero pollution, making them an eco-friendly alternative to traditional building materials. Additionally, each tile contains one day's worth of clean air, making it a valuable product in terms of improving indoor air quality.

Tejas Sidnal's innovation is not only environmentally friendly, but it also creates new opportunities for sustainable economic growth. The use of carbon waste as a raw material for making tiles can create a new industry, providing jobs and boosting local economies. It also offers an opportunity for businesses to adopt sustainable practices, reduce their carbon footprint, and improve their reputation.

However, there are also some challenges to be overcome in the production and adoption of these tiles. The manufacturing process is still in its early stages and may require further research and development to make it more efficient and cost-effective. Additionally, the initial cost of these tiles may be higher than traditional building materials, making them less accessible to the general public.

In conclusion, Tejas Sidnal's innovation of turning carbon waste into tiles is a game-changer in the field of sustainable construction. It offers a sustainable solution to the problem of pollution while also creating value-added products. The use of carbon waste as a raw material can create new opportunities for sustainable economic growth, making it a win-win situation for both the environment and the economy. As more and more people become aware of the importance of sustainable practices, the demand for these tiles is likely to increase, leading to further research and development in this field. The future of sustainable construction is bright, and innovations like these tiles are paving the way for a cleaner and greener future.

The Solar-Powered Speedster: How One African Kid Beat Elon Musk at His Own Game

Emmanuel is an inspiration to many people worldwide, not only in Sierra Leone but also across the African continent and beyond. He is a testament to the power of imagination and determination, and his story is one of resilience, creativity, and ingenuity.

Emmanuel's journey started with a problem that he identified in his community: the harmful effects of car pollution on the environment and people's health. He realized that the traditional cars that people were using were emitting fumes that were causing respiratory problems, allergies, and even cancer. He wanted to find a solution to this problem, but he faced a significant obstacle: he had no money to finance his project.

Despite this setback, Emmanuel did not give up. Instead, he decided to use something that he had in abundance: his imagination. He started to envision a car that would not emit any fumes, would not require any fuel, and would be made entirely from recycled materials. He scoured junkyards, collected scrap metal, cane sticks, old cables, and wires, and started to assemble his dream car.

The process of building the car was not easy, and it took Emmanuel three years of hard work and perseverance to bring his imagination to life. However, he never gave up, and he kept working on the car every day, even when it seemed like the project was impossible.

Finally, Emmanuel's dream car was born. He called it the "Imagination Car" or "Magnesium Car" because it was everything he had imagined it to be. He painted it with the colors of his country, green, white, and blue, and added doors, headlights, brakes, and even a horn. The car runs entirely on solar power, and it can reach a speed of up to 15 kilometers per hour.

Emmanuel's car is not only an impressive feat of engineering, but it is also a symbol of hope and possibility. It shows that even with limited resources and no financial backing, it is possible to create something amazing and valuable.

Emmanuel's story is also a reminder that the solutions to Africa's problems do not necessarily have to come from Europe or America. Africans themselves have the talent, creativity, and ingenuity to find solutions to the challenges they face. Emmanuel's invention is proof of this, and he is just one of many African innovators who are making a difference in their communities and beyond.

The impact of Emmanuel's invention goes beyond the car itself. It has inspired many people, especially young people, to think creatively and innovatively about solving problems in their communities. Emmanuel's story is a powerful example of the role that innovation and technology can play in improving people's lives and creating a better future.

Emmanuel's dream does not end with the Imagination Car. He has many more ideas for environmentally friendly products that can reduce pollution, noise, and clean the environment. He dreams of building products that can make a real difference in people's lives, and he is committed to pursuing his goals, no matter how difficult the journey may be.

In conclusion, Emmanuel's story is an inspiring example of what is possible when we use our imagination, creativity, and determination to solve problems and make a difference in the world. His invention is not only an impressive engineering feat but also a symbol of hope, possibility, and the power of African innovation. Emmanuel's journey reminds us that we can all make a difference, no matter how small or big, and that the solutions to our problems may be closer than we think.

The Free Travel Guru: How One Man Hacked the Credit Card System and Never Paid for a Flight Again

Credit card rewards programs have become increasingly popular over the years, offering consumers the opportunity to earn points or cash back for their purchases. For some, these programs are a way to save money and get more value for their spending. For others, they are a way to travel for free or stay in luxury hotels without having to pay anything out of pocket.

One individual who has taken credit card rewards to the extreme is Chris, who has accumulated over 12 million credit card points over the last 20 years. Chris started his journey into credit card rewards when he began working in a bank after college. He quickly realized that the banks were making a lot of money from credit card transactions and that they were incentivizing people to use their credit cards by offering rewards programs.

Chris began tracking the bonuses and rewards offered by different credit cards in a spreadsheet on his computer. He would look for credit cards that offered the most rewards for different categories such as groceries, gas, and travel, and would use these cards for his purchases. Over time, he accumulated millions of credit card points that he could use to travel for free.

To earn these rewards, Chris had to open many different credit card accounts and keep track of each card's requirements for earning points.

He also had to keep track of the expiration dates for his points and make sure to use them before they expired.

Chris is not alone in his quest for credit card rewards. Many people have found ways to maximize their rewards and earn free travel and other perks. However, there are risks associated with using credit cards to earn rewards, including getting into debt or overspending in order to earn rewards.

Credit card rewards can be a double-edged sword, and it's important to use them wisely. For those who are responsible with their credit card use, rewards programs can offer a great way to earn free travel, hotel stays, and other perks. However, those who are not careful can quickly find themselves in debt and struggling to make payments.

To use credit card rewards wisely, it's important to start by choosing the right cards. Look for cards that offer rewards in categories that you frequently spend money on, such as groceries or gas. It's also important to read the fine print and understand the terms and conditions of each card before applying.

Once you have your cards, it's important to use them responsibly. Only use your credit cards for purchases that you can pay off in full each month. Avoid carrying a balance on your cards, as this can quickly lead to debt and high interest charges.

To maximize your rewards, it's also important to take advantage of special promotions and bonus offers. Many credit card companies offer sign-up bonuses for new customers, as well as bonuses for spending in specific categories or on certain purchases. By taking advantage of these offers, you can quickly earn a lot of points or cash back.

Finally, it's important to keep track of your rewards and use them before they expire. Many rewards programs have expiration dates for points or miles, so it's important to stay on top of your rewards and use them before they disappear.

In conclusion, credit card rewards programs can offer a great way to earn free travel, hotel stays, and other perks. However, it's important to use them responsibly and avoid overspending or getting into debt. By choosing the right cards, using them responsibly, and taking advantage of special promotions and bonus offers, you can maximize your rewards and enjoy the benefits of credit card rewards programs.

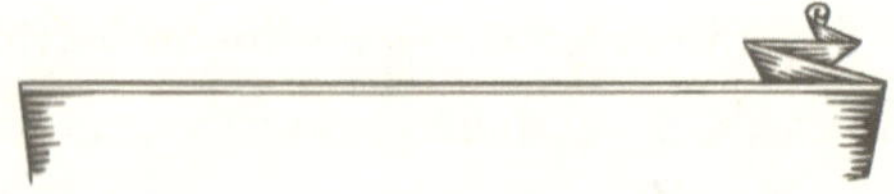

The Yellow Mellow Fellow

Abu Zakur, the man who only wears yellow, is an intriguing figure that has gained popularity in Aleppo, Syria, for his unique fashion sense. He has been wearing yellow clothing for almost 40 years, including yellow shoes, ties, jackets, pyjamas, and even a yellow clock. Despite the ongoing war in Syria, Abu Zakur continues to walk the streets wearing his bright and bold yellow outfits, bringing joy and positivity to those around him.

Abu Zakur's story is inspiring because of his resilience and the way he chooses to express himself. In a country torn apart by war, his bright and cheerful demeanour serves as a beacon of hope for those around him. His love for the colour yellow stems from the idea that it represents sunshine and happiness, and he wants to spread that positivity wherever he goes. He has become an icon in Aleppo, and people often stop him on the street to take selfies with him or simply to say hello.

However, Abu Zakur's unique fashion sense has also made him a target of criticism and even violence. Some people in Aleppo have compared him to Donald Trump, and there is a statue of him in the city. Still, when rebels took over the city in 2012, Abu Zakur was attacked and advised to stop wearing yellow. Despite the danger, he continues to wear yellow because it represents something positive to him.

Abu Zakur's story highlights the importance of individual expression and how it can have an impact on others. Despite the societal pressures to conform and fit in, Abu Zakur has chosen to stay true to himself and his love for the colour yellow. His choice has not only brought joy to himself but also to the people around him. His story is a reminder that being different can be a good thing and can inspire others to be true to themselves as well.

In a world that often values conformity and uniformity, Abu Zakur's story reminds us of the beauty of individuality. He is a symbol of hope and positivity, and his fashion sense has become a part of his identity. He is a reminder that we should embrace our uniqueness and that it can have a positive impact on the world around us.

Moreover, Abu Zakur's story also illustrates the resilience of the human spirit. Despite living in a country that has been plagued by war and violence for many years, Abu Zakur continues to spread positivity and joy through his unique fashion sense. He has not let the chaos around him dampen his spirits, but rather has chosen to stay true to his beliefs and values.

Finally, Abu Zakur's story is a testament to the power of social media and the internet in spreading positive messages and stories. The video documenting Abu Zakur's story has been viewed by thousands of people around the world, and his story has been shared on various social media platforms. His message of positivity and individuality has resonated with people from all walks of life and has inspired many to embrace their uniqueness.

In conclusion, Abu Zakur's story is an inspiring tale of individuality, resilience, and the power of positivity. His love for the colour yellow has become a part of his identity, and he has chosen to express himself through his unique fashion sense despite the dangers and pressures around him. His story is a reminder that being different can be a good thing and can inspire others to be true to themselves as well. Abu Zakur's story is an excellent example of the importance of embracing our individuality and spreading positivity and joy wherever we go.

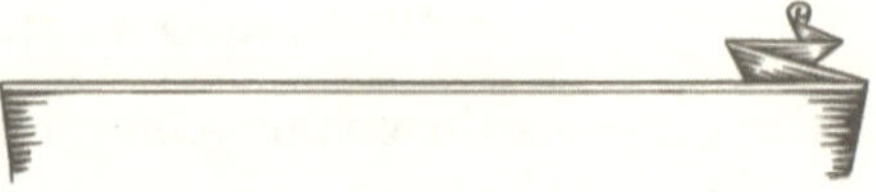

The First Woman to Reach the Top of the World (Literally)

Raha Moharrak, the first Saudi Arabian woman to climb Mount Everest, has become an inspiration for women all over the world. Her achievement is an example of how women can overcome negative attitudes and stereotypes to reach their goals. Her story is not just about climbing a mountain, but also about breaking barriers and challenging cultural norms.

Raha's journey to the top of Mount Everest was not an easy one. She had to overcome obstacles that were not just physical but also cultural. In Saudi Arabia, women are often limited in their choices and opportunities. They are expected to stay at home, take care of the family, and not pursue their dreams. Raha's decision to climb Mount Everest was seen as an unusual and risky move, especially for a woman.

Raha's determination and perseverance helped her to overcome the challenges she faced. She trained hard for the climb, both physically and mentally. She walked long distances in heavy boots, carried a heavy backpack, and prepared herself for the harsh conditions of the mountain. She had to deal with snowstorms, freezing temperatures, and altitude sickness. She even had to go for days without simple things like water, showers, and warm food. But she did not let any of these challenges stop her from reaching her goal.

Raha's climb to the top of Mount Everest is not just a personal achievement but also a symbolic one. It shows that women can break cultural norms and achieve things that were once considered impossible. Raha's success has inspired many other women in Saudi Arabia and other parts of the world to pursue their dreams, no matter how challenging they may seem.

Raha's story is also a reminder of the importance of gender equality and the need to remove barriers that limit women's opportunities. In many countries, women still face discrimination and inequality in education, employment, and other areas of life. They are often denied basic rights and freedoms, which limits their potential and hinders their ability to contribute to society.

Raha's climb to the top of Mount Everest is a testament to the power of determination and the human spirit. It shows that anything is possible if we have the courage to pursue our dreams and overcome the obstacles in our way. Raha's story is not just about climbing a mountain but also about breaking barriers, challenging cultural norms, and inspiring others to do the same.

In conclusion, Raha Moharrak's climb to the top of Mount Everest is an incredible achievement that has inspired women all over the world. Her story is not just about climbing a mountain but also about breaking barriers and challenging cultural norms. It is a reminder of the importance of gender equality and the need to remove barriers that limit women's opportunities. Raha's success has shown that anything is possible if we have the courage to pursue our dreams and overcome the obstacles in our way. Her story will continue to inspire generations of women to come.

The Cube Commander: Leading the Charge in Rubik's Revolution

Rubik's Cube is a fascinating puzzle that has intrigued millions of people all around the world. This 3D puzzle is a challenging and entertaining way to test one's problem-solving skills. However, for some people, the Rubik's Cube is not just a toy or a puzzle but an art form. Such is the case of Giovanni Contardi, a Rubik's Cube artist who has gained international recognition for his unique and beautiful portraits made out of hundreds of Rubik's Cubes.

Giovanni's journey began when he was just 15 years old, and a friend introduced him to the Rubik's Cube. He was fascinated by the puzzle and learned to solve it in under 10 seconds, which is an impressive feat. However, he soon got bored with solving the cube repeatedly and decided to do something more creative with it.

Giovanni's idea of using the Rubik's Cube as an art medium was not an easy task. It took him a lot of trial and error to figure out how to mix hundreds of Rubik's Cubes to create beautiful and detailed portraits. Each portrait required many months of work, and one bad cube could ruin the entire picture. Moreover, once the Rubik's Cubes were glued and framed, they became incredibly heavy. Despite these challenges, Giovanni persisted, and his hard work paid off.

Today, Giovanni is known worldwide for his Rubik's Cube art. His portraits are in high demand, and celebrities like Will Smith and The Rock have shared his work on social media. Giovanni's art has also been featured in galleries and exhibitions worldwide.

The rise of Rubik's Cube art is not just limited to Giovanni. There are many other artists who have explored the creative potential of the Rubik's Cube. One such artist is New York-based, CubeWorks Studio. This studio creates large-scale murals, sculptures, and installations entirely out of Rubik's Cubes. The studio's work has been featured in many high-profile events and exhibitions, including the Smithsonian American Art Museum.

The popularity of Rubik's Cube art has led to an increased interest in the Rubik's Cube as an art medium. There are many online communities and forums dedicated to Rubik's Cube art, where artists can share their work, exchange ideas, and collaborate on new projects. These communities have helped to create a supportive environment for Rubik's Cube artists, encouraging them to explore new creative possibilities.

Apart from Rubik's Cube art, the Rubik's Cube has also found use in other creative fields. For example, the Rubik's Cube has been used as a teaching tool for mathematics and geometry. Educators have found that using the Rubik's Cube in the classroom helps students to develop critical thinking skills and spatial reasoning.

In recent years, the Rubik's Cube has also been used in scientific research. Scientists have used the Rubik's Cube to study cognition, memory, and problem-solving skills. For example, researchers at the University of Amsterdam used the Rubik's Cube to study visual perception and memory. The study found that expert Rubik's Cube solvers were better at recognizing patterns and remembering the position of the cubes than non-expert solvers.

Moreover, the Rubik's Cube has also been used in robotics research. Scientists have developed robots that can solve the Rubik's Cube using machine learning algorithms. These robots can solve the Rubik's Cube in a matter of seconds, which is faster than any human can.

In conclusion, the Rubik's Cube has evolved from a simple puzzle to a versatile tool that can be used for art, education, research, and entertainment. The rise of Rubik's Cube art has opened up new creative possibilities, inspiring artists worldwide to explore the potential of this unique puzzle. As the Rubik's Cube continues to captivate people's imagination, we can expect to see more exciting developments in the future.

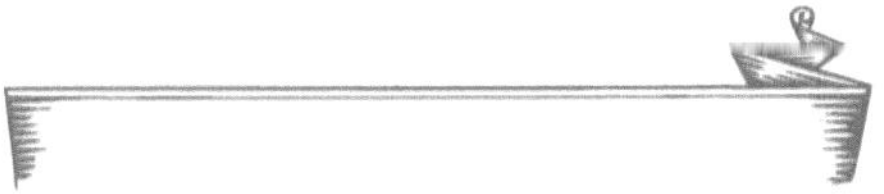

The Last Supper: A Fugu Feast to Remember (or Not)

Fugu is a type of pufferfish, and it is one of the most dangerous foods in the world. The fish contains a potent toxin called tetrodotoxin, which is 1,200 times more toxic than cyanide. The toxin is found in the ovaries, liver, and other organs of the fish, and it can cause paralysis and death within minutes if ingested in sufficient quantities. Because of this, only licensed chefs are permitted to prepare and serve fugu in Japan.

Serving fugu requires years of training and certification. Chefs must undergo a rigorous apprenticeship that can last up to ten years, during which they learn the art of fugu preparation and develop the necessary skills to safely remove the toxic parts of the fish. Once they have completed their training, they must pass a test that includes both a written exam and a practical demonstration of their skills.

Despite its deadly reputation, fugu is a delicacy in Japan, and it has been enjoyed for centuries. The fish is typically served as sashimi, or raw fish sliced thinly and arranged artistically on a plate. To prepare fugu sashimi, the chef must carefully remove the skin, bones, and other organs of the fish, leaving only the edible flesh. The flesh is then sliced into thin pieces and arranged on a plate with garnishes such as shiso leaves, grated radish, and soy sauce.

While fugu is expensive, with prices ranging from $30 to $200 per person, it is considered a status symbol among many Japanese diners. Eating fugu is a sign of wealth and sophistication, and it is often served at formal events such as weddings and business meetings. In addition to sashimi, fugu can be prepared in a variety of other dishes, including tempura, soup, and hot pot.

While fugu is generally safe to eat when prepared by a licensed chef, there have been incidents of people becoming ill or dying from improperly prepared fish. In 2018, two men died after eating fugu liver that had been illegally sold by an unlicensed vendor in Osaka. In response to this incident, the Japanese government tightened regulations on fugu sales and increased penalties for unlicensed vendors.

In addition to Japan, fugu is also consumed in other parts of Asia, including Korea and China. However, the fish is much less popular outside of Japan, and it is often considered too dangerous to be served in other countries. In the United States, for example, the sale and preparation of fugu are heavily regulated, and only a handful of restaurants are licensed to serve the fish.

In conclusion, fugu is one of the most dangerous foods in the world, and it requires extensive training and certification to prepare and serve safely. Despite its deadly reputation, fugu is considered a delicacy in Japan, and it has been enjoyed for centuries. While there are risks associated with eating fugu, many Japanese diners are willing to take those risks for the chance to enjoy this unique and delicious dish.

Paper Planes: Not Just for Kids Anymore

John Collins, also known as "The Paper Airplane Guy," is a master of paper airplane design and has been perfecting his designs for over 40 years. His passion for flying objects began when he was a child, and he has since become an expert in the field of paper airplane design.

Collins emphasizes that the key to a successful paper airplane is precision. Each fold and crease must be accurate to ensure the desired flight pattern is achieved. He has studied the physics of real airplanes to replicate their mechanics in his paper airplane designs, and he believes that each paper airplane throw is like a science experiment. Collins has used his paper airplanes as tools for scientific experimentation, and he hopes to inspire others to do the same.

Despite his success in the field, Collins is not a scientist or engineer. He is simply a grown-up kid who never stopped being curious. He believes that his success is a testament to the power of curiosity and the importance of never losing the desire to learn and explore.

In addition to being a skilled paper airplane designer, Collins has also broken the Guinness World Record for the longest paper airplane flight. His airplane traveled 69.14 meters in nine seconds, which is the length of a football stadium. He achieved this with a simple eight-fold design, which he named after his wife, Suzanne.

Collins sees paper airplanes as more than just toys. He believes that they have the potential to be used as a tool for scientific experimentation, and he hopes to inspire others to pursue their curiosity and explore the possibilities of simple objects like paper airplanes.

The story of John Collins is a reminder of the power of curiosity and the importance of pursuing one's passions. Despite not being a scientist or engineer, Collins has become an expert in his field through years of hard work and dedication. His success serves as a testament to the idea that anyone can achieve their goals if they are willing to put in the effort and never lose their desire to learn and explore.

Collins' story also highlights the importance of simplicity. In a world where technology and complexity are often seen as the keys to success, Collins has achieved great things with a simple sheet of paper. He reminds us that sometimes the simplest things can be the most powerful, and that we should never overlook the potential of everyday objects.

Overall, John Collins' story is a powerful reminder of the importance of curiosity, hard work, and simplicity. His success in the field of paper airplane design serves as an inspiration to anyone who has ever pursued a passion, and his belief in the power of simple objects is a refreshing perspective in a world that often values complexity above all else.

The Human Stock Exchange: Meet the First Publicly Traded Person

The story of Mike, the man who sold his life, is a thought-provoking example of the intersection of technology and human agency. His decision to sell shares in his life on the internet for a dollar each raises questions about the ethics of selling one's life and allowing others to control personal decisions. However, it also highlights the potential for innovation and new forms of social and economic organization in the digital age.

At its core, Mike's decision to sell shares in his life is a radical experiment in self-commodification. By dividing his life into shares and inviting people to buy them, he effectively turned himself into a tradable asset. This approach has precedent in the world of art and performance, where artists have used their bodies and personal lives as a medium for creative expression. However, Mike's project takes this idea to a new level by inviting anyone with an internet connection to participate in the creation and direction of his life.

The implications of this kind of project are vast and multifaceted. On one hand, it challenges traditional notions of ownership and control. Mike's shareholders have a say in his personal decisions, but he retains some agency over how he executes those decisions. This creates a unique power dynamic that raises questions about the nature of consent and autonomy in the digital age. It also blurs the line between the private and the public, as personal decisions become subject to shareholder voting and public scrutiny.

At the same time, Mike's project highlights the potential for new forms of social and economic organization in the digital age. The internet has created new opportunities for peer-to-peer collaboration and collective decision-making, and Mike's project is an example of how these tools can be applied to personal life. By selling shares in his life, Mike is essentially creating a new kind of market that is driven by collective decision-making rather than individual ownership. This opens up possibilities for new forms of governance and economic activity that are more democratic and inclusive.

However, the project also raises important ethical questions about the potential risks and pitfalls of this kind of experimentation. For example, what happens if future investors are not as understanding as Mike's current shareholders? What if they demand decisions that compromise his well-being or infringe on his rights? What if they want to take the project in a direction that he does not agree with? These are all important questions that need to be considered when experimenting with new forms of social and economic organization.

Overall, Mike's project is an example of the complex and nuanced ways in which technology is changing the nature of human agency and decision-making. It challenges traditional notions of ownership and control, while also highlighting the potential for new forms of collaboration and economic activity. However, it also raises important ethical questions that need to be carefully considered in order to ensure that these kinds of experiments are conducted in a responsible and sustainable manner.

Chalk It Up to Innovation: The Blackboard Computer

Richard's story is a testament to the power of education and the impact that a dedicated teacher can have on the lives of his students. Born and raised in a poor town in Ghana, Richard grew up without access to technology, but his first encounter with a computer left a lasting impression on him. He recognized the immense potential of this little box to change the world and decided to become a computer science teacher to share that knowledge with others.

However, when Richard started teaching, he realized that his students could not afford computers. This was a common problem in many parts of the world where access to technology was limited due to economic constraints. In order to teach his students, Richard had to think creatively and come up with alternative solutions. He did not have access to computers, but he did have a blackboard and chalk, and he decided to draw a computer screen on the board.

Richard drew each part of the computer, including the mouse, monitor, and cable, until his blackboard looked exactly like a Microsoft Word window. His students would follow his lead, step-by-step, and copy his work to learn how to use the software. While it wasn't a perfect solution, Richard was providing his students with the knowledge they needed to compete with others around the world. He knew that if his students could learn how to use technology, they would have more opportunities in the future.

Richard's story is not unique. Many teachers around the world face similar challenges when it comes to teaching technology to students who don't have access to computers. This is especially true in developing countries where poverty and lack of infrastructure are major obstacles. However, Richard's dedication and ingenuity are a shining example of how teachers can make a difference despite these challenges.

The digital divide is a global issue that affects millions of people. According to a report by the International Telecommunication Union, almost half of the world's population is still not using the internet. This is a staggering statistic, given the many benefits that technology can offer. The internet has revolutionized the way we live and work, and it has opened up new opportunities for education, healthcare, and economic growth. However, these benefits are not evenly distributed, and many people are left behind.

The digital divide has many causes, including poverty, lack of infrastructure, and political barriers. In many developing countries, the cost of technology is prohibitive, and many people cannot afford to buy a computer or pay for internet access. This creates a vicious cycle where lack of access to technology leads to fewer opportunities for education and economic growth, which in turn perpetuates poverty and inequality.

To address the digital divide, governments, non-governmental organizations (NGOs), and private companies have launched various initiatives to increase access to technology in developing countries. These initiatives include providing free or low-cost computers and internet access, building infrastructure, and investing in education and training programs. While these efforts have made some progress, much more needs to be done to close the digital divide.

In addition to infrastructure and access, another important factor in addressing the digital divide is education. Teachers like Richard play a critical role in educating students about technology and how to use it. However, many teachers themselves lack the training and resources they need to teach technology effectively. This is especially true in developing countries where resources are limited, and training programs are often unavailable.

To address this issue, many organizations have launched training programs and initiatives to support teachers in developing countries. For example, the United Nations Educational, Scientific, and Cultural Organization (UNESCO) has launched several initiatives to improve technology education in developing countries, including providing training to teachers and developing educational materials. Other organizations, such as the One Laptop per Child (OLPC) initiative, have focused on providing low-cost laptops to children in developing countries to improve access to technology.

While these efforts are commendable, there is still much work to be done to bridge the digital divide and ensure that every child has access to the technological tools necessary for success in the 21st century. One major challenge is the lack of funding for these initiatives. Many developing countries simply do not have the resources to invest in technology education or to provide students with the necessary equipment. In some cases, governments may be hesitant to invest in technology education due to other pressing social and economic issues.

Another challenge is the lack of infrastructure to support technology education. In many developing countries, schools may not have access to reliable electricity or internet connectivity, which makes it difficult to provide students with the tools they need to learn about and use technology. Even in cases where equipment has been donated or provided, it may be difficult to maintain and repair due to a lack of resources or technical expertise.

In addition, there is a need for culturally-relevant technology education programs that take into account the unique needs and perspectives of students in developing countries. For example, many students in rural areas may have different experiences with technology than their urban counterparts. They may also have different cultural beliefs and practices that need to be taken into account when designing technology education programs.

To address these challenges, a multi-faceted approach is needed. Governments, non-governmental organizations, and private companies all have a role to play in bridging the digital divide and promoting technology education in developing countries. This may involve investing in infrastructure, providing training and educational resources to teachers, and partnering with local organizations to develop culturally-relevant technology education programs.

One promising area for innovation is the use of mobile technology to provide educational resources and support to students in developing countries. With the widespread availability of smartphones and mobile internet connectivity, there is an opportunity to provide students with access to educational materials and resources that were previously unavailable. For example, organizations like eLimu in Kenya have developed mobile applications that provide students with access to interactive educational content, including videos, quizzes, and games.

Another potential solution is the use of open-source software, which can be freely distributed and adapted to meet the unique needs of different communities. For example, the Learning Equality initiative has developed a platform called Kolibri that provides educational resources, including textbooks, videos, and interactive exercises, that can be accessed offline and adapted to meet the needs of different communities.

Ultimately, bridging the digital divide and promoting technology education in developing countries will require sustained commitment and investment from governments, NGOs, and private companies. However, the potential benefits are significant. By providing students with access to technology and the skills they need to use it effectively, we can help to promote economic development, improve health outcomes, and reduce poverty in some of the world's most vulnerable communities.

The Pastor, The Box, and The Babies: A Tale of Love, Compassion, and a Hole in the Wall

The story of Pastor Lee's baby box is one that tugs at the heartstrings and sheds light on a deeply troubling issue: the abandonment of new-born babies. In South Korea, and indeed many other countries, it is unfortunately not uncommon for mothers to leave their new-born babies in unsafe places or to dispose of them altogether. Pastor Lee's baby box, therefore, has become a beacon of hope for both the abandoned babies and their mothers.

The inspiration for the baby box came from Pastor Lee's personal experience. His own child was born with complications, and he spent a lot of time in hospitals. It was during this time that he began to notice the large number of abandoned babies, and the realization that he needed to do something to help them took root. The baby box was born out of this need to provide a safe space for babies to be left, without judgment or repercussions.

The baby box itself is a small hole in the wall, located at the side of Pastor Lee's church. It is designed to be easy to use, with a simple lever that opens the door to the box. Once a baby is placed inside, an alarm sounds to alert Pastor Lee or one of his volunteers, who can then collect the baby within seconds. The baby is then taken to a safe place where it can be cared for and given the medical attention it needs.

It's important to note that the baby box is not just a one-stop solution for abandoned babies. Rather, it is a part of a broader initiative that aims to support both the babies and their mothers. Pastor Lee provides financial assistance to mothers who are struggling, as well as counselling and emotional support. He works to empower them and help them to feel supported, so that they can make the best decisions for themselves and their babies.

Over the years, Pastor Lee has saved around 1,600 babies, a truly remarkable feat. His efforts have not gone unnoticed, and he has received recognition and praise from people all over the world. However, his work is not without its detractors. Some people have criticized the baby box, arguing that it encourages mothers to abandon their babies rather than seeking help. Others have raised concerns about the legality of the baby box, as it exists outside of the legal framework for adoption in South Korea.

Despite these criticisms, however, Pastor Lee remains committed to his cause. He believes that the baby box is an important tool in the fight against infant abandonment and that it is ultimately saving lives. Moreover, he sees the baby box as a symbol of hope and compassion in a world that can often be harsh and unforgiving.

The story of Pastor Lee's baby box is a powerful reminder of the importance of compassion and empathy in our lives. It shows us that even in the face of great tragedy, there is always hope, and that small acts of kindness can have a profound impact on the world around us. It is a testament to the power of community and the strength of the human spirit. Ultimately, the story of Pastor Lee and his baby box is a story of love, and it is one that deserves to be told and celebrated.

The Matriarchal Oasis: Where Women Rule and Men Drool

The story of Umoja village in Kenya is a powerful example of how women can build a society, lead, run businesses, and thrive if given the chance. In many parts of the world, women face significant obstacles in accessing education, healthcare, and economic opportunities, as well as in their personal relationships and interactions with men. This often leads to situations of violence, discrimination, and poverty, perpetuating a cycle of oppression and marginalization.

Rebecca Lolosoli's story begins with her experience of being in an abusive marriage. She was beaten and treated like a second-class citizen, and when she asked the authorities to protect her, no one helped. This experience is unfortunately common for many women around the world, where domestic violence and gender-based violence are prevalent but often go unreported or unaddressed by authorities.

Rebecca's response to this situation was to create a village where women could live without men. This was a radical idea that challenged gender norms and patriarchal structures that dominate many societies around the world. By creating Umoja, Rebecca and her fellow women were able to build a community that was centred around their own needs, desires, and goals, without having to worry about the constraints and limitations imposed on them by men.

Umoja is not just a physical space; it is also a symbolic one. It represents a vision of a world where women can be free to pursue their own dreams and aspirations without being held back by the expectations of others. It is a place where women can support each other, learn from each other, and empower each other to be the best versions of themselves.

However, Umoja has not been without its challenges. The men in neighbouring villages were initially jealous of the women's success and tried to undermine them by blocking tourists from visiting Umoja and even physically attacking them. The women in Umoja were able to resist these attempts and eventually bought out the entire men's village, showing that they were capable of not only surviving but thriving in a world without men.

The story of Umoja is a testament to the power of women to create change and build communities that are centred around their own needs and desires. It is also a reminder of the challenges that women face in societies where gender norms are deeply entrenched and patriarchal structures dominate. To create a world where women can succeed, governments need to make better policies to protect and give more chances to women, and parents need to educate their sons to respect women.

One way to achieve this is through education. By providing women with access to quality education, they can acquire the skills and knowledge they need to pursue their dreams and contribute to their communities. Education can also help women become more aware of their rights and empower them to speak out against violence and discrimination.

Another way to support women is by creating economic opportunities for them. This can be done by providing women with access to credit, training, and mentorship, as well as by promoting women's entrepreneurship and encouraging more women to enter traditionally male-dominated fields. When women have access to economic opportunities, they can become more independent and less reliant on men for financial support.

It is also important to address the root causes of gender inequality, such as discriminatory laws and policies, social norms, and attitudes. This can be done through advocacy and awareness-raising campaigns that challenge traditional gender roles and promote gender equality. It can also involve working with men and boys to change their attitudes and behaviours towards women and girls.

In conclusion, the story of Umoja village in Kenya is a powerful reminder of the potential of women to create change and build communities that are centred around their own needs and desires. It is also a call to action for governments, parents, and individuals around the world to support women's rights and empower women to succeed.

A Bus, a Boat, and a Dream: How One Man Travelled to Every Country Without Flying

Thor Pedersen is a Danish adventurer who embarked on an extraordinary journey to visit every country in the world without ever taking a flight. He achieved this feat in a journey that lasted 1,426 days and spanned over four years, traveling through 195 countries. This was an extraordinary achievement, given that the vast majority of international travellers choose air travel to reach their destinations.

Thor's journey started in October 2013 when he left his hometown of Denmark with just a pair of shoes and a backpack. He was determined to travel the world by land and sea, and he did just that. His mode of transportation varied from buses, trains, container ships, trucks, and even a horse carriage. He spent an average of just $20 per day on his travels, a testament to his resourcefulness and ability to travel on a tight budget.

Thor's journey was not without challenges. He had to deal with visa problems, accommodation issues, and long stretches of time on board container ships, where he would spend several weeks at sea with no land in sight. He also had to navigate conflict zones, risking his life on several occasions.

One particularly harrowing experience occurred when he was traveling through Cameroon to Congo. In the middle of the night, his vehicle was stopped by three uniformed men who were armed and drunk. Thor feared for his life and thought that he would be shot.

However, he was able to convince them to let him pass and continue on his journey.

Despite the many obstacles that he encountered along the way, Thor never lost sight of his goal. He was determined to be the first person to visit every country in the world without flying. His passion for travel, his desire to see the world, and his determination to succeed kept him going through the toughest times.

Thor's journey also allowed him to experience the world in a way that few people have. He was able to immerse himself in different cultures, taste local cuisine, and meet people from all walks of life. He saw some of the most beautiful landscapes on earth, from the mountains of South America to the beaches of the Maldives. His journey was an adventure of a lifetime, and it changed him in ways that he never could have imagined.

Thor's achievement has inspired many people around the world to travel more, see more, and experience more. His journey showed that travel can be a transformative experience that changes the way we see the world and ourselves. He proved that it is possible to travel on a tight budget and that we do not need to rely on air travel to see the world.

Thor's journey also highlights the importance of perseverance, determination, and hard work. His achievement was not an overnight success but the result of years of planning, preparation, and hard work. He never lost sight of his goal, even when things got tough, and he was willing to do whatever it took to achieve it.

In conclusion, Thor Pedersen's journey to visit every country in the world without flying is an extraordinary achievement. His journey highlights the importance of perseverance, determination, and hard work, and shows that it is possible to travel on a tight budget. His passion for travel, his desire to see the world, and his determination to succeed are an inspiration to us all.

The Beard That Defied Gravity: The Story of the World's Best Facial Hair

The story of MJ Johnson and his beard is one of perseverance, dedication, and following one's dreams. It is a testament to the power of hard work and determination and how they can lead to success and recognition. But it is also a story that resonates with many people because it highlights the importance of embracing one's uniqueness and pursuing one's passions, no matter how unconventional they may seem.

MJ's interest in competitive beard growing started when he saw a photo of the World Beard and Mustache Championship, which he describes as "so weird, so ridiculous, so crazy" that he was immediately drawn to it. Despite not having any prior experience with beard growing or competitions, he decided to give it a try and set his sights on winning first place. And so, he put away his razor and started growing his beard, focusing on perfecting his style and achieving the unique look that would impress the judges.

It was not an easy journey, however. MJ's first attempts at growing an epic beard were met with ridicule and criticism from others who thought he was crazy or looked horrendous. But MJ did not let this deter him. Instead, he persevered and kept working hard, trying again and again until he achieved the look he was after. And after four years of hard work, he finally won a beard competition, marking the beginning of a new chapter in his life.

MJ's beard not only won him the admiration of the world but also opened up new opportunities for him. His beard appeared in media all over the world, on beard products that were sold in the US, ads on trucks in Europe, and even on newspapers in Asia. He also got to travel and join beard clubs around the world, making lifelong friends along the way. He says that his beard has been "a really, really cool amazing passport to the world," and he does not know where he would be without it.

But more than just winning competitions and gaining recognition, MJ's story is a reminder that pursuing one's passions and following one's dreams can lead to unexpected and incredible outcomes. His message is that even if you are not good at something at first, you should still try because you never know where it might lead you. By giving 110% effort and not giving up, you might just achieve something great and life-changing.

MJ's story is not just about beard growing or competitions. It is about the power of perseverance and determination, the importance of embracing one's uniqueness, and the potential of pursuing one's passions. His story can inspire others to take risks, step outside of their comfort zones, and pursue their dreams, no matter how unconventional or difficult they may seem.

In a world where conformity and fitting in are often valued more than individuality and standing out, MJ's story is a refreshing reminder of the beauty and power of embracing one's uniqueness. It shows that being different can lead to incredible opportunities and recognition, and that pursuing one's passions can bring immense joy and fulfillment.

Moreover, MJ's story highlights the importance of having a supportive community and being surrounded by like-minded people who share your passions and interests. Through his involvement in beard clubs and competitions, MJ was able to meet people from all over the world who shared his love for beards and who supported and encouraged him along the way.

Finally, MJ's story is a reminder of the potential of the internet and social media to connect people from all over the world and to provide a platform for individuals to share their passions and interests. It is through social media and the internet that MJ's beard gained worldwide recognition, and it is through these platforms that many people are able to connect with others who share their interests and passions.

In conclusion, the story of MJ Johnson and his beard is a powerful reminder of the importance of embracing one's uniqueness, pursuing one's passions, and never giving up on a dream. It is a story that inspires us to think outside the box, to take risks, and to work hard to achieve our goals. MJ's journey teaches us that success is not always about talent or natural ability, but rather about dedication, persistence, and the willingness to push through failure and setbacks.

Breadcrumbs and Bird Brains: The Story of India's Feathered Friend

Joseph Sega, also known as the Generous Birdman of India, has become an inspiration for many people around the world because of his selfless act of feeding 4,000 birds every day for the last 16 years. Joseph's story is an excellent example of how one individual can make a difference in the world, no matter how small it may seem. His dedication to helping these birds is truly remarkable, and it shows how even the smallest acts of kindness can have a significant impact on the world around us.

Joseph's journey began in 2004, when a devastating tsunami hit Chennai, India, leaving many people and animals homeless. As a result, many birds were forced to migrate to find a new source of food. Joseph's house was one of the few places that had food, and soon, four birds started coming to his roof to eat. The next day, the four birds brought their friends, and the number of birds visiting Joseph's roof started to increase rapidly.

Feeding 4,000 birds every day is not an easy task, and it requires a lot of dedication and hard work. Joseph pays for the birds' food from his own pocket, and he spends 50 rupees every day to buy rice to feed them. This may not seem like a lot, but it's roughly 40% of his daily expenses. Joseph wakes up every morning at 4:30 am, goes to the market to buy rice, cooks it, and spreads it on planks on his roof. Thousands of birds then flock to his house to eat.

Joseph has been doing this twice a day, every day for the last 16 years, no matter the weather. He has not left his house for 27 years, and his dream is to buy the house one day and continue feeding the birds until he passes away. Joseph's dedication to this cause is truly remarkable, and it shows how one person's selfless act of kindness can have a ripple effect on the world around us.

Joseph's story is not just about his dedication to feeding the birds; it's also about the relationship between humans and nature. In many parts of the world, urbanization and development have led to a decrease in natural habitats for birds and other animals. Joseph's act of feeding the birds shows that humans can coexist with nature and help to preserve the environment.

In addition to his impact on the environment, Joseph's story has also had a significant impact on people around the world. His selflessness and dedication have inspired many people to start their own acts of kindness, no matter how small they may seem. His story has become a beacon of hope in a world that often seems bleak and hopeless.

Joseph's story is also a reminder of the power of individual action. Often, we feel powerless to make a difference in the world, and we wait for someone else to take action. Joseph's story shows that even one individual can make a difference and that small acts of kindness can have a significant impact on the world around us.

In conclusion, Joseph Sega's story is not just about feeding birds; it's about the power of individual action, the relationship between humans and nature, and the impact that one person can have on the world. His selfless act of kindness has inspired people around the world, and it's a reminder that even the smallest acts of kindness can make a significant impact. Joseph's story is a testament to the power of human compassion and the potential for positive change in the world.

Fixing More Than Wires: The Inspiring Tale of John, the Free House Fixer

John is an electrician with a heart of gold who has inspired many people with his kindness and generosity. His story is one of selflessness, compassion, and a determination to make the world a better place for those who are less fortunate.

John's story began when he received a call from an old lady who needed help fixing a light in her home. When he arrived, he found that the house was in a state of disrepair, with half the lights not working, the water not running, and animals getting inside. The lady had no family members to help her, and she was too old to realize how bad the situation had become.

Instead of simply fixing the light and leaving, John decided to take matters into his own hands. He gathered a group of friends and volunteers and set about fixing up the entire house for free. However, as they worked, they realized that there was more to be done than they could handle alone. They needed to buy materials and supplies, and they needed more help from the community.

To raise the necessary funds and support, John turned to the internet and created a Facebook page called "Nice Old Lady Needs Help." The response was overwhelming. People from all over the country and the world were moved by the story of this single old lady in Minnesota, and they wanted to help.

In less than a month, John raised over $115,000. With that money, he and his team were able to replace everything in the house, from the lights to the windows, and even the backyard and porch steps. The old lady's broken house was transformed into a welcoming home where she could spend her retirement years.

The story of John and the old lady quickly went viral, with news outlets picking up the story and contractors from all over the country calling to offer their services. John's act of kindness had sparked a ripple effect, inspiring others to help those in need.

But John wasn't done yet. He realized that there were many other old people out there who needed help but didn't have the resources or support to get it. So, he decided to turn his one-man operation into a national campaign to help old people.

He gathered construction workers and volunteers from all over the country, calling the group "Gloria's Gladiators" after the old lady's name. Any old person who didn't have the resources to repair their home could reach out to the group for help.

John's story is a powerful example of the impact that a single act of kindness can have. He started with a simple act of fixing a light, but that act of kindness snowballed into something much bigger, inspiring others to come together and help those in need.

What makes John's story so inspiring is that he didn't do it for fame or recognition. He did it simply because he saw someone in need and wanted to help. His selflessness and compassion have touched the lives of many, and his legacy will continue to inspire others to make a positive difference in the world.

The QWERTY Picasso: Typewriter Art That Will Blow Your Mind

Art is an expression of creativity that has been a part of human history since prehistoric times. Over time, art has evolved in form, style, and medium. From cave paintings to sculptures, from canvas to digital media, art has always been a reflection of the artist's thoughts, emotions, and experiences. Gurumurthy, a typewriter artist from Bangalore, India, is an excellent example of how art can transcend traditional mediums and take on new forms.

Gurumurthy's art is unique in that he creates it using a typewriter, a machine that was primarily designed for typing letters and documents. He uses the keys of the typewriter to create art by typing letters and numbers in a specific pattern, which forms the image. Gurumurthy's art is a testament to the idea that creativity has no bounds, and that innovation can lead to extraordinary results.

The idea of creating art using a typewriter might seem bizarre, but it is not entirely new. Typewriter art, also known as "typewritten art," has been around for decades. In the past, artists used typewriters to create artworks, poems, and other forms of creative writing. However, Gurumurthy has taken the concept of typewriter art to a new level by creating complex portraits and drawings using only the keys of a typewriter.

Gurumurthy's journey as a typewriter artist began when he was a banker, and he used his typewriter for work. He would often use his free time to make drawings with traditional art tools like paints and brushes. One day, while sitting in front of his typewriter, he had a sudden idea. What if he used his typewriter to create artwork? He experimented with the idea by typing letter after letter, key after key, until he created his first typewriter artwork, a portrait of Robert Kennedy.

Gurumurthy's first artwork was a success, and he continued to experiment with the idea, creating more intricate portraits and drawings. His artwork gained popularity on social media and was shared widely on national television. Gurumurthy's unique artwork has made him a well-known figure in India and beyond.

One of the significant challenges of creating art on a typewriter is the lack of an erase button or backspace. Once a mistake is made, it cannot be corrected, and the artist must start over. Gurumurthy has overcome this challenge by perfecting his technique and ensuring that his keystrokes are precise and accurate.

Gurumurthy's artwork is a prime example of how creativity and innovation can lead to new forms of expression. His art is not only unique but also inspiring. Gurumurthy's dedication to his craft is admirable, and his art has been recognized by many, including politicians and prime ministers.

Gurumurthy's journey as a typewriter artist is a testament to the power of passion and perseverance. His art has inspired many, and he continues to create new works of art, pushing the boundaries of what is possible with a typewriter. Gurumurthy's work shows that art can be created from any medium, as long as there is creativity and imagination.

In conclusion, Gurumurthy's story as a typewriter artist highlights the power of creativity and innovation. His unique artwork is a testament to the idea that art can be created from any medium, and that with passion and perseverance, anything is possible. Gurumurthy's story serves as an inspiration for artists everywhere, encouraging them to experiment with new forms and mediums of art. As technology continues to evolve, it will be fascinating to see how artists like

Gurumurthy use new tools and techniques to create even more innovative works of art.

The Feathered Feast: A Poultry Alternative

Sorawut's innovative approach to making meat from chicken feathers is a significant breakthrough in the food industry. With the increasing demand for meat, this invention could provide an alternative to traditional meat sources, reducing the environmental impact of meat production and addressing the issue of food scarcity.

The global meat industry is a significant contributor to greenhouse gas emissions, land degradation, and water pollution. According to the United Nations, the meat industry contributes to 18% of global greenhouse gas emissions, more than the entire transportation sector. The meat production process is also highly water-intensive, using up to 15,000 liters of water to produce one kilogram of beef. In addition, the meat industry requires large areas of land to raise animals, leading to deforestation and habitat loss. Sorawut's invention could help reduce the environmental impact of meat production by providing an alternative source of protein that requires fewer resources to produce.

Moreover, Sorawut's invention could help address the issue of food scarcity. With a growing global population and increasing demand for meat, traditional meat production may not be sustainable. According to the United Nations, the world population is expected to reach 9.7 billion by 2050, requiring a 70% increase in food production. With limited resources, it may not be possible to meet this demand through traditional meat production. Therefore, alternative sources of protein, such as Sorawut's chicken feather meat, could help bridge the gap between food demand and supply.

Another benefit of Sorawut's invention is the reduction of food waste. In traditional meat production, parts of the animal that are not used for human consumption are discarded, leading to food waste. Sorawut's approach to using chicken feathers as a source of meat reduces waste by utilizing a part of the chicken that would otherwise be thrown away. By using feathers to make meat, Sorawut is creating a circular economy, where waste is minimized, and resources are reused.

However, there are potential challenges to the adoption of Sorawut's chicken feather meat. One challenge is the acceptance of this type of meat by consumers. Some people may find the idea of eating meat made from feathers unappetizing or unappealing. However, Sorawut's approach to making the meat look and taste like traditional chicken meat may help overcome this barrier. Moreover, it may take some time for people to accept this type of meat as a viable alternative to traditional meat sources.

Another potential challenge is the cost of producing chicken feather meat. While Sorawut's invention reduces waste and utilizes a part of the chicken that would otherwise be discarded, the cost of production may be higher than traditional meat sources. However, as the demand for alternative sources of protein increases, the cost of production may decrease, making it more affordable and accessible.

In conclusion, Sorawut's invention of making meat from chicken feathers is an innovative approach to address the challenges of traditional meat production, including environmental impact, food scarcity, and food waste. While there may be challenges to its adoption, this invention has the potential to provide a sustainable and viable alternative to traditional meat sources. By utilizing resources that would otherwise be discarded, Sorawut's approach is a step towards a more circular and sustainable food system.

The Flash of Fractions: The Life and Times of The Fastest Human Calculator

Scott Flansburg is a man who has defied convention in his approach to learning and mathematics. As the world's fastest human calculator, he is capable of adding numbers faster than he can speak. But what sets him apart from others is not just his ability to perform rapid calculations, but his unconventional approach to learning and his unique way of looking at numbers.

Flansburg's journey began in third grade when he was punished for not paying attention in math class. His teacher called him up to the board and asked him to solve a math problem. Rather than getting into trouble, Flansburg surprised his teacher by coming up with the correct answer without any preparation. This turned out to be the start of a journey that would see him become one of the world's most accomplished mental calculators.

As Flansburg progressed through school, he began to develop a new way of counting. Instead of thinking of numbers as being from one to ten, he realized that if you think of them as being from zero to nine, it becomes easier to visualize the number grid and perform mental arithmetic. Additionally, he discovered that when performing calculations in your head, it is much more efficient to work from left to right rather than right to left, as you can keep a running total and avoid the need for carrying.

Using these methods, Flansburg began to develop his own approach to mathematics. He discovered fun patterns and easy tricks for counting, and his unique brain became a deadly combination. Before he knew it, he had become the fastest human calculator in the world, according to the Guinness World Record, not once but twice, despite never attending college or graduating from high school.

But Flansburg's journey didn't end there. He realized that many students find math boring because of the way it is taught, and so he decided to take it upon himself to make math more accessible and fun for students. He began visiting schools, showing kids that math is not as complicated as they might think and using everyday examples to illustrate the importance of numbers.

For Flansburg, numbers are the most precise, powerful, and popular language on the planet. His mission is to help students see how numbers are all around us in everyday life and how important they are in making decisions, whether it's buying a car, leasing a car, or managing a bank account.

Flansburg's story is an inspiration to anyone who has struggled with math or felt that it was too complicated. He shows that there is always more than one way to learn, and that sometimes you just need to make your own rules. He also demonstrates the power of perseverance and the importance of finding your own path in life.

Beyond his remarkable abilities in mental arithmetic, Flansburg's story also highlights the importance of a growth mindset and the need for educators to be more flexible and creative in their teaching methods. Too often, students are taught in a rigid, one-size-fits-all manner that fails to account for the unique strengths and learning styles of each individual. By taking an unconventional approach to learning, Flansburg was able to unlock his own potential and inspire others to do the same.

In a world that is becoming increasingly reliant on technology and automation, the ability to think critically and creatively is more important than ever. Flansburg's approach to learning and his love of numbers show that there is still much that we can learn from the human mind and the power of human imagination. As we look to the future, we must continue to cultivate these qualities in ourselves and in future generations if we are to meet the challenges that lie ahead.

In conclusion, Scott Flansburg's story is an inspiration to anyone who has struggled with math or felt that it was too complicated. He demonstrates the power of perseverance and the importance of finding your own path in life. But beyond his remarkable ability to calculate numbers quickly, there are important lessons we can learn from Scott's approach to learning and teaching math.

The Crop Farmer Who Planted a Hospital

The story of Karimul Haque is a remarkable example of how one person can make a significant impact on society despite facing challenging circumstances. Born and raised in a remote village in India, Karimul faced the harsh realities of living in a region that lacked basic amenities, including proper medical facilities. When his mother fell seriously ill, Karimul was forced to take her to a hospital that was located a great distance away. This experience left an indelible impression on him, as he realized that many people in his village faced similar challenges when it came to accessing medical care.

Determined to make a difference, Karimul began using his motorbike to transport sick people to the hospital for free. He turned his motorbike into a makeshift ambulance, using it to transport patients over rough terrain and through difficult weather conditions. At first, many people in his village laughed at him, but he persisted, knowing that he was doing something valuable and necessary. Over time, his efforts began to bear fruit, and he saved many lives that would have otherwise been lost due to the lack of medical care.

As word of his efforts spread, people from all over the world began to take notice of Karimul's work. He received donations from many generous individuals, which he used to build a free hospital in his village. This hospital has since become a lifeline for people who live in the area, providing them with access to quality medical care that was previously unavailable. Moreover, Karimul has continued to use his motorbike to transport sick people to the hospital, even during the COVID-19 pandemic, when many other healthcare workers were too afraid to do so.

Karimul's story is one that should inspire all of us to do more for our fellow human beings. Despite being born into a world that did not offer him many opportunities, he has managed to make a significant impact on society. He did not let his circumstances define him, but instead used them as motivation to create change. His story also highlights the importance of access to quality healthcare, especially in remote areas that are often overlooked by policymakers and healthcare professionals.

There are several lessons that we can learn from Karimul's story. First, we should always strive to help those who are less fortunate than us, regardless of the challenges we may face. Second, we should never give up on our dreams, no matter how difficult they may seem. Third, we should recognize the importance of community and work together to create a better future for all of us. Finally, we should remember that we are all capable of making a difference, no matter how small or insignificant our actions may seem.

The story of Karimul Haque also raises important questions about the state of healthcare in India, particularly in rural areas. According to a 2021 report by the World Health Organization, India has one of the lowest ratios of healthcare workers to population in the world, with just 0.7 doctors and 1.7 nurses per 1,000 people. Moreover, many rural areas lack basic medical facilities, and people often have to travel long distances to access care. This situation has been exacerbated by the COVID-19 pandemic, which has overwhelmed the country's healthcare system and left many people without access to care.

To address these challenges, policymakers in India and other countries must invest more resources in healthcare infrastructure, particularly in rural areas. This includes building more hospitals and clinics, recruiting and training more healthcare workers, and investing in technologies that can improve access to care, such as telemedicine. At the same time, there is a need to recognize the contributions of people like Karimul, who are often the unsung heroes of healthcare. These individuals demonstrate the power of community-led healthcare initiatives, which can be just as effective, if not more so, than traditional healthcare systems.

Ultimately, Karimul's story serves as a reminder that healthcare is a collective responsibility, and that everyone has a role to play in ensuring that all individuals have access to the care they need to lead healthy and fulfilling lives. Whether it is through building hospitals, providing training and resources to healthcare workers, or engaging with communities to identify and address healthcare needs, we all have a part to play in building a more equitable and just healthcare system.

Around the World in 1,400 Days: A Woman's Quest for Global Domination

Cassie De Pecol's journey to become the first woman to travel solo to every country in the world and the fastest person ever to do so is an incredible achievement that deserves recognition and admiration. Her journey took three years to plan, secure visas, find sponsors, investors and map out her entire trip. Cassie's incredible feat was not only an adventure of a lifetime, but it was also an opportunity to promote peace, understanding, and unity.

Throughout the video, Cassie talks about her motivation to travel the world alone, leave all preconceptions at the door, and have her own experience about countries that she visited around the world without any outside sources telling her what she should feel or think about that place. Her desire to explore different cultures, traditions, and ways of life on a global scale was a way of breaking down the barriers of stereotypes and prejudice that people have towards other cultures.

Despite warnings about the dangers of the big bad world, including the risk of rape, beatings, or even death, Cassie decided to face her fears by doing something no woman has ever done before. She set out to visit all 196 countries in the world alone and to beat every man by being the fastest person to do so.

Cassie's journey was not without its challenges. She had to adhere to strict Guinness World Record rules, including not spending more than 14 days in any country, and having physical proof of being in all countries, including North Korea. The trip was also costly, with her raising funds from sponsors, investors, and donors to finance her trip. Despite the challenges, Cassie persisted in her pursuit of this incredible achievement.

As a woman, Cassie faced unique challenges on her journey. She had to be aware of her surroundings, keep in touch with friends and family, and stay safe. However, she found that people all over the world were kind and hospitable, and she saw that humanity was beautiful. Cassie's journey taught her that people from different cultures and backgrounds all share similar needs and desires, such as the need for a roof over their heads, a hot meal, and someone to love.

Cassie's journey to become the first woman to visit every country alone is an inspiration to women all over the world. Her journey shows that with determination, perseverance, and the right mindset, anything is possible. It also highlights the importance of breaking down barriers between cultures and promoting unity and understanding between people.

Cassie's incredible feat shows that women can achieve anything they set their minds to, and they should be encouraged to pursue their dreams, break records, and do things better than anyone else in the world. By breaking down barriers and promoting peace and understanding, women like Cassie can become ambassadors of peace, goodwill, and inspiration for generations to come.

In conclusion, Cassie De Pecol's journey to become the first woman to travel solo to every country in the world and the fastest person ever to do so is a remarkable achievement that deserves recognition and admiration. Her journey was not only an adventure of a lifetime, but it was also an opportunity to promote peace, understanding, and unity. By breaking down barriers and promoting peace and understanding, women like Cassie can become ambassadors of peace, goodwill, and inspiration for generations to come.

The Gender Bender: A Woman's Quest for Masculinity

Gender roles and expectations vary significantly across cultures, and for many women in patriarchal societies, opportunities for education, work, and independence are often limited. However, the story of Rihanna from Pakistan, who defied societal expectations by becoming a taxi driver, demonstrates the power of determination and resilience.

From a young age, Rihanna wanted to be a man because she believed that men were strong, powerful, and independent. She played with boys and emulated their behaviour, but as she grew older, her family urged her to conform to traditional gender roles and become a wife and mother. Despite this pressure, Rihanna remained determined to control her own destiny and pursue her dreams.

Unfortunately, a tragic accident left Rihanna alone to care for her three children, and her husband left her. Faced with financial hardship and social ostracization, Rihanna decided to enter the man's world and become a taxi driver. This was a significant challenge, as taxi driving was a job that was almost exclusively reserved for men in Pakistan.

Nevertheless, Rihanna persevered and became one of the first women in her country to become a taxi driver. She was able to earn a steady income, pay off her house rent, and live independently. In doing so, she not only defied traditional gender roles, but she also inspired many other women to follow in her footsteps and pursue careers that were traditionally reserved for men.

Rihanna's story highlights the importance of resilience and determination in the face of adversity. It also underscores the need for greater gender equality in society. Women like Rihanna should have the same opportunities as men to pursue their dreams and achieve financial independence. However, achieving gender equality is not always easy, and it requires a concerted effort by individuals, communities, and governments.

One significant obstacle to gender equality is the persistence of gender stereotypes and societal expectations. In many societies, women are still expected to be the primary caregivers and homemakers, while men are expected to be the breadwinners. These gender roles and expectations are often deeply ingrained in culture and reinforced by family, friends, and the media.

To overcome these obstacles, it is essential to challenge and disrupt traditional gender roles and expectations. This can be done through education and awareness-raising campaigns that promote gender equality and encourage men and women to pursue careers and activities that challenge gender norms. It can also be achieved through policy and legal reforms that promote equal opportunities for women in education, employment, and politics.

Another critical factor in achieving gender equality is the need to address gender-based violence and discrimination. Violence against women is a widespread problem in many societies, and it is often a barrier to women's economic and social empowerment. Addressing this issue requires a comprehensive approach that includes legal and policy reforms, education and awareness-raising campaigns, and support services for survivors of violence.

Finally, achieving gender equality requires the involvement of both men and women. Men must be encouraged to take an active role in promoting gender equality and challenging gender stereotypes. They can do this by supporting women's rights, advocating for gender-sensitive policies, and modelling non-violent and equitable behaviour. Women, on the other hand, must be encouraged to speak out and assert their rights. They can do this by advocating for their own rights, supporting other women, and promoting gender equality in their communities.

In conclusion, the story of Rihanna from Pakistan is a powerful example of the resilience and determination required to overcome gender-based discrimination and societal expectations. Her decision to become a taxi driver challenged traditional gender roles and inspired other women to pursue careers that were traditionally reserved for men. However, achieving gender equality requires a concerted effort by individuals, communities, and governments to challenge gender norms, address gender-based violence and discrimination, and promote equal opportunities for all.

The White Gold Rush: A Tale of Salt, Sweat, and Tears

Salt, a simple yet essential ingredient in our daily lives, has played a significant role in human history for thousands of years. It was used not only as a seasoning for food, but also as a preservative for meat and fish, a currency for trade, and a symbol of wealth and power. In many ancient civilizations, salt was even considered sacred and used in religious ceremonies.

The process of salt-making has evolved over time, from early methods of collecting salt from natural sources such as saltwater ponds, salt springs, and salt mines, to more advanced techniques of salt extraction and purification using machines and factories. With the development of modern technology and transportation, salt has become more widely available and affordable than ever before.

However, the traditional practice of salt-making, which involves manual labour and a deep connection to the natural environment, is slowly disappearing. Juan, the salt maker from a remote mountain village in Mexico, is one of the last practitioners of this ancient craft. His job is to make salt using his hands and feet, a process that requires patience, skill, and an intimate knowledge of the land and its resources.

For Juan and his ancestors, salt-making has been a way of life for generations. They have passed down their knowledge and expertise from father to son, mother to daughter, and have created a rich cultural tradition that is deeply rooted in the community. However, as the world becomes more industrialized and urbanized, fewer young people are interested in pursuing a career in salt-making, which is seen as old-fashioned, difficult, and unprofitable.

The decline of traditional salt-making is not only a loss of cultural heritage, but also a threat to the environment and our health. Most of the salt that we consume today is heavily processed and contains additives such as anti-caking agents, iodine, and fluoride, which can have negative effects on our bodies if consumed in large amounts. In contrast, natural salt, such as the one made by Juan, is free of these additives and contains trace minerals that are essential for our health and well-being.

As more people become aware of the benefits of natural and organic food, there is a growing demand for products such as natural salt, which is not only healthier but also more flavorful and aromatic. However, meeting this demand requires a different approach to salt-making, one that is sustainable, environmentally friendly, and socially responsible.

To achieve this, we need to support and promote small-scale salt-makers like Juan, who use traditional methods that are gentle on the environment and create jobs and income for local communities. We also need to invest in research and development to improve the efficiency and quality of natural salt production, and to explore new ways of adding value to this precious resource.

Furthermore, we need to raise awareness among consumers about the benefits of natural salt and the risks associated with processed salt. This can be done through education campaigns, labelling requirements, and certification programs that recognize and promote the use of natural salt in food products.

In conclusion, the story of Juan, the last salt maker in Mexico, is not just about salt making, but about the importance of preserving cultural heritage, protecting the environment, and promoting healthy and sustainable food practices. By supporting small-scale salt-makers and promoting natural salt, we can help to ensure that this precious resource continues to enrich our lives for generations to come.

Lunar Landlord: Meet the Man Who Rules the Moon

The story of Chris Lamar and the Lunar Embassy is a fascinating one that raises many questions about the ownership of extra-terrestrial property and the legality of selling it to people around the world. Chris's father's idea to own real estate on the moon came from his desire to own property on Earth, which was too expensive. However, he found a loophole in the 1967 Outer Space Treaty that stated that no governmental or sovereign entity has any ownership rights over celestial bodies within our solar system. This treaty did not mention individuals, so Chris's father wrote a letter to the United Nations declaring the moon was his, and he started selling properties on the moon.

Chris and his father have been selling properties on the moon for over 41 years and have claimed to own 200 million acres of the moon. They have divided this portion into 5 million small properties and sold them to people worldwide, including celebrities, corporations, and past presidents. Their business model is simple; they have a proprietary grid system that is very methodical and gives buyers exact coordinates of their property. They also have a registration database that keeps track of everyone's position, and every property that they sell comes with a prime view of the Earth.

The prices of these properties are relatively affordable and range from $25 to $500. This affordability makes it possible for anyone to buy property on the moon and other celestial bodies in the solar system. Chris and his father have even expanded their business to include properties on Mercury, Mars, Venus, the Moon of Earth, and Io, one of Jupiter's moons. The fact that they have been able to sell properties on the moon and other celestial bodies for over 41 years is a testament to their business acumen.

However, the legitimacy of their business is questionable as they are not a government. Chris's father created his own government just to sell stuff on the moon, which is not recognized by any other government. This lack of recognition raises many legal questions, and it is unclear whether their business is legal or not. The fact that they are not a government also means that they have no control over the land that they claim to own. The moon and other celestial bodies are subject to international space law, which means that no one can own them.

The United Nations Outer Space Treaty of 1967 is the main international treaty that governs activities in space. It states that the exploration and use of outer space should be carried out for the benefit of all countries and that no country can claim ownership of outer space or any celestial body. This means that any claim of ownership over the moon or any other celestial body by Chris and his father is not legally valid.

There are also practical issues with owning property on the moon. The lack of atmosphere on the moon means that it is exposed to space radiation, extreme temperatures, and micrometeoroids. This means that any property on the moon would require significant investment in infrastructure to make it habitable. The cost of transporting materials and building structures on the moon would be prohibitively expensive, and it is unlikely that anyone would be able to afford it.

In conclusion, the story of Chris Lamar and the Lunar Embassy raises many questions about the ownership of extra-terrestrial property and the legality of selling it to people around the world. While their business model may be profitable, it is not legally valid, and the lack of recognition from any government means that they have no control over the land that they claim to own. The moon and other celestial bodies are subject to international space law, which means that no one can own them. Therefore, owning property on the moon or any other celestial body is currently not a realistic or legal option.

The Mouldy Mystery: A Roommate's Love Affair with Rotting Food

In today's world, where climate change and environmental degradation are pressing issues, there are people like Lorena who are going to great lengths to live sustainably and reduce their environmental footprint. This is an important movement towards protecting the planet and preserving its resources for future generations. By adopting eco-friendly practices in their daily lives, people like Lorena are making a positive impact on the environment.

Lorena's eco-friendly practices are varied and comprehensive. One of the things she does is to take short cold showers. This is a simple yet effective way to conserve water and energy, and it is something that everyone can do. Collecting water from showers to reuse in the toilet is another effective way to conserve water. By doing this, Lorena is reducing her water usage and conserving a precious resource.

Another eco-friendly practice that Lorena follows is deleting unnecessary emails to save energy and server space. This might seem like a small thing, but when millions of people do it, it can have a significant impact on the environment. By reducing the energy usage of servers, we can reduce the amount of greenhouse gases emitted into the atmosphere.

Lorena is also careful about the food she consumes and the waste it generates. She collects food waste from her friends to compost, ensuring that none of it goes to waste. This is an effective way to reduce food waste, which is a significant problem globally. Food waste not only wastes resources but also emits greenhouse gases as it decomposes. By composting food waste, Lorena is reducing the amount of greenhouse gases emitted into the atmosphere.

Lorena also carries a handkerchief instead of using tissues. This is a small yet effective way to reduce paper waste, which is another significant problem. By reducing paper waste, Lorena is helping to preserve trees and other natural resources. She refuses to use plastic and brings her own cutlery and containers, which is another effective way to reduce waste.

Using a rock deodorant instead of a plastic one is another eco-friendly practice that Lorena follows. This is an effective way to reduce plastic waste, which is a significant problem globally. Plastic waste takes hundreds of years to decompose, and it is causing significant environmental problems. By using a rock deodorant, Lorena is reducing the amount of plastic waste that she generates.

Lorena also only buys second-hand clothes, which is an effective way to reduce waste and preserve resources. The fashion industry is one of the most polluting industries globally, and buying second-hand clothes is an effective way to reduce the demand for new clothes. This, in turn, reduces the resources used in the production of new clothes and reduces the amount of waste generated.

Finally, Lorena contacts companies to suggest changes to their products. This is an effective way to promote sustainability and reduce waste. By suggesting changes to products, Lorena is encouraging companies to adopt eco-friendly practices, which can have a significant impact on the environment.

In conclusion, Lorena's eco-friendly practices are varied and comprehensive. By adopting these practices, she is making a positive impact on the environment and reducing her environmental footprint. We can all learn from Lorena and adopt eco-friendly practices in our daily lives to protect the planet and preserve its resources for future generations. This is a pressing issue, and it is up to all of us to take action and make a difference.

Madness at the Clown Motel: A Horror Story in Real Life

The Clown Motel in Tonopah, Nevada is a popular destination for those who are fascinated by creepy clowns and are seeking a unique, quirky experience. The motel is owned by Vijay and Hamee Anand, who have created a world-famous collection of clown dolls and memorabilia over the years.

The Anands bought the motel for $800,000 in 1995, and it had already been operating for over 50 years. The motel had a reputation for being run-down and had a location next to an old cemetery, which didn't appeal to most people. However, the Anands saw the potential to turn the motel into something unique and special.

When they first took over the motel, it had only 800 clown dolls, but now it has over 2,000. People from all over the world have donated clown dolls, paintings, pictures, statues, and postcards, making the collection even more impressive. Some people even come to the motel just to donate their clown memorabilia to the collection.

Despite the creepy ambiance of the motel, Vijay and Hamee take great pride in the cleanliness and safety of their establishment. They work hard to ensure that the motel is a safe and comfortable place for their guests to stay, even with the abundance of clown dolls that could potentially scare some visitors.

The Anands have capitalized on the motel's creepy reputation by embracing it and even making it scarier. They have added more clown dolls and decorations to the motel, making it a surreal experience for those who stay there. The rooms are decorated with clown wallpaper, and there are clown dolls everywhere, even in the bathrooms.

However, the Anands' creativity doesn't stop at the decorations. They have also created some unique amenities to add to the overall experience of the motel. For example, the motel has a graveyard next door, and the Anands offer a "ghost hunt" experience for those who are brave enough to explore the cemetery at night.

The Anands have also added a small chapel next to the motel, which has become a popular location for weddings. Couples who are looking for a unique wedding location can exchange their vows surrounded by clown dolls and other memorabilia.

Despite the motel's popularity, there are some who find it too creepy and avoid it altogether. The Anands understand this and have tried to keep the clown decorations contained to specific areas of the motel, so guests can avoid them if they choose to.

The Clown Motel has gained a lot of media attention over the years, with many publications, websites, and television shows featuring it. The motel has even been used as a filming location for movies and television shows, including the Travel Channel's "Ghost Adventures."

The Clown Motel is an example of how one person's passion and creativity can turn a run-down motel into a popular tourist attraction. Vijay and Hamee Anand have created a unique experience for their guests, and they take great pride in the success of their establishment. The motel may not be for everyone, but for those who are seeking a creepy and unforgettable experience, it's definitely worth a visit.

Blind Ambition: From Home Cook to Master Chef

Christine Ha's story is a testament to the power of resilience and determination in the face of adversity. Despite losing her vision in her 20s, Christine refused to let her disability define her, and instead, she adapted her cooking techniques and developed a unique system to enable her to continue pursuing her passion for cooking.

As a blind chef, Christine had to learn how to cook using her other senses, such as taste and sound. She also developed a highly organized system for her kitchen, where she would arrange all her tools and ingredients in specific places, making it easier for her to locate everything. This approach required a great deal of planning and preparation, as she had to know exactly where everything was, which required her to be meticulous and well-organized.

Despite the challenges, Christine persevered and continued to hone her culinary skills. Her dedication and talent led her to compete in a cooking competition against able-bodied chefs, where she wowed the judges with her unique approach to cooking. Her lack of vision, which could have been a disadvantage, turned out to be an advantage, as she had developed a heightened sense of taste and was able to create dishes that were both delicious and visually stunning.

Christine's success as a blind chef is an inspiration to all, but it is especially important for people with disabilities. Her story shows that with determination and creativity, anything is possible, and that one's disability does not have to be a barrier to success. Christine's message is one of hope, and she is an example of what can be achieved when one sets their mind to something.

In addition to her culinary achievements, Christine is also an advocate for people with disabilities. She believes that the term "disabled" is not an accurate reflection of people's abilities, and instead, she prefers the term "differently-abled." This shift in language reflects her belief that everyone has unique talents and abilities, and that we should celebrate our differences rather than focus on our limitations.

Christine's story also highlights the importance of accessibility in society. As a blind person, she faced many challenges in her daily life, from navigating public spaces to finding employment opportunities. Her experience highlights the need for society to be more inclusive and accommodating to people with disabilities, so that they can fully participate in all aspects of life.

In conclusion, Christine Ha's story is a powerful reminder of the resilience and determination that can overcome adversity. Despite losing her vision, she continued to pursue her passion for cooking, and her unique approach to the culinary arts has inspired people around the world. Her message of hope and inclusivity is a powerful one, and her story serves as an example of what can be achieved when we embrace our differences and work towards a more accessible and inclusive world.

The G.O.A.T. (Greatest of All Time) Herder: A Tale of Unstoppable Confidence and Cuteness

The story of the Chinese girl who leads 300 goats is a testament to the value of alternative forms of education. It challenges the traditional notion that education can only happen within the four walls of a classroom and highlights the importance of allowing children to explore and learn from the world around them.

In the context of artificial intelligence (AI), this story is particularly relevant. AI has the potential to revolutionize the way we approach education, by providing personalized learning experiences that cater to individual students' needs and interests. However, this requires a shift in our understanding of what constitutes education, and a willingness to embrace alternative approaches to learning.

One of the key benefits of AI in education is its ability to personalize learning experiences. Traditional classroom settings often operate on a one-size-fits-all approach, with students expected to learn at the same pace and in the same way. However, this approach is not always effective, as students have different learning styles, interests, and strengths. AI can help address this issue by using data analytics to identify students' strengths and weaknesses, and tailoring learning experiences accordingly.

For example, AI-powered platforms like DreamBox and Knewton use adaptive learning algorithms to adjust the difficulty level of questions based on students' previous responses. This allows students to work at their own pace and level, without feeling bored or overwhelmed. Similarly, AI-powered chatbots like Duolingo's language tutors can provide personalized feedback and guidance to students, helping them to improve their language skills in a way that is tailored to their individual needs.

AI can also help to bridge the gap between formal and informal education. The story of the Chinese girl who leads 300 goats highlights the value of learning from real-world experiences, rather than just textbooks and lectures. AI can help facilitate this type of learning by creating immersive, interactive simulations that allow students to explore and learn from different scenarios.

For example, virtual reality (VR) and augmented reality (AR) technologies can provide students with realistic, interactive simulations of real-world environments. This can be particularly useful for subjects like science and history, where students can explore different concepts and events in a more engaging and memorable way. Similarly, AI-powered chatbots and voice assistants can provide students with access to information and resources outside of the classroom, helping to supplement their formal education with informal learning opportunities.

However, there are also challenges and potential pitfalls associated with using AI in education. One of the main concerns is that AI-powered systems may reinforce existing biases and inequalities. For example, if the data used to train an AI system is biased, it may perpetuate these biases in its recommendations and decision-making. Similarly, if AI-powered platforms are not accessible to all students, it may exacerbate existing inequalities in education.

Another challenge is the potential for AI to replace human teachers. While AI can provide personalized learning experiences and facilitate learning in new and innovative ways, it cannot replace the human connection and support that teachers provide. It is therefore important to find a balance between using AI to enhance and supplement education, while still valuing and supporting the role of human teachers.

In conclusion, the story of the Chinese girl who leads 300 goats highlights the importance of embracing alternative forms of education, and the potential of AI to support and enhance these approaches. By using AI to personalize learning experiences, bridge the gap between formal and informal education, and provide new and innovative ways of learning, we can create a more effective and engaging education system that caters to the needs and interests of all students. However, it is important to be mindful of the potential pitfalls and challenges associated with using AI in education, and to ensure that these technologies are used in a way that promotes equity, accessibility, and human connection.

WORCESTERSHIRE: The Word That Broke the Internet

English is a challenging language, even for those who speak it as their first language. For those learning it as a second or third language, the challenges are even greater. Pronunciation is a particular challenge, and words like "Worcestershire" and "anti-disestablishmentarianism" can be daunting to pronounce. This is where experts like Jack Hi Noss come in. Jack has been the pronouncer for the spelling bee competition in the US for 18 years, and he has an incredible talent for spelling and pronunciation.

The English language is a complex one. It is a combination of different influences, including Latin, French, and Greek, each with their own spelling systems. This has led to many different ways of spelling the same sound, such as the letters "gh" being pronounced as "f" in "enough" or skipped altogether in "knight". The schwa sound, which is an "uh" sound, is also a particular challenge for spellers, as it can be made by any vowel or the letter "y".

In addition to spelling, the meaning and origin of words are also important. Jack Hi Noss recommends that spellers learn the meaning and origin of words, as this can help them figure out how to spell them. He also suggests that learners work hard and practice every day, especially on simple words. Simple monosyllabic words are the most powerful ones, according to Jack, and they are often used by the best writers.

The spelling bee competition in the US is a popular event that showcases the talents of young spellers. Children learn all the words in the dictionary and go on stage to listen to Jack pronounce a word and try to spell it correctly. The competition is a combination of brute force memorization and analytical thinking. Jack believes that the secret to mastering English is a combination of these two approaches.

For non-native speakers of English, the challenges of learning the language can be even greater. However, with hard work and practice, it is possible to become proficient in English. One way to do this is by focusing on simple words and learning their meaning and origin. Another way is to find patterns in the language that can help with spelling and pronunciation.

In conclusion, English is a challenging language, but with the help of experts like Jack Hi Noss, it is possible to become proficient in spelling and pronunciation. Learning the meaning and origin of words can also be helpful, as can focusing on simple monosyllabic words. The spelling bee competition in the US is an excellent showcase for young spellers and provides an opportunity for them to learn and improve their skills. For non-native speakers, hard work and practice are key to mastering English.

Cigarette City: How One Man Transformed His Island with a Million Butts

Megicho is a remarkable person whose life story is both inspiring and thought-provoking. Despite the many challenges he faced, he persevered and transformed his life in ways that most people would find impossible. His journey teaches us that it's never too late to turn your life around, no matter how difficult the circumstances may be.

Megicho's life began with tragedy when his mother passed away in an earthquake just three days after he was born. His father was too poor to send him to school, so Megicho grew up without any formal education. However, a rich man promised his father to school him in the Galapagos Islands. But he was abandoned on a boat in the middle of the ocean to survive. This experience alone could have been enough to break anyone's spirit, but Megicho was determined to make the best of his situation.

Despite the hardships he faced, Megicho became a fisherman and started to believe in life. However, he faced another test of his resilience when his engine died while he was on his boat, leaving him alone to survive in the middle of the ocean for 77 days. After being rescued, he was sent to jail for not being able to pay back his debts. This experience caused him to become depressed and an alcoholic for 12 years.

Many people would have given up on life at this point, but Megicho didn't. At the age of 52, he decided to turn his life around. He learned how to read by himself, so he could train his mind. He started eating healthy, learned how to jog, bike, and lift to train his body. With hard work and dedication, he became so strong that he ran a marathon at age 68.

However, Megicho's story doesn't end there. He fell in love with nature and wanted to clean his island, so he started collecting cigarette butts on the streets every day. After five years, he collected one million cigarette butts and turned them into works of art. These sculptures made him famous on his tiny island and around the world.

Megicho's journey is a testament to the power of the human spirit. He faced numerous obstacles in his life, but he refused to give up. Instead, he worked hard and transformed his life in ways that most people would find impossible. His story is an inspiration to anyone who is struggling with their own challenges.

There are many lessons that we can learn from Megicho's life. One of the most important is that it's never too late to turn your life around. No matter how difficult your circumstances may be, you can always make a change for the better. Megicho started at the age of 52, but there's no reason why you can't start right now.

Another lesson we can learn from Megicho's story is the importance of resilience. Megicho faced numerous setbacks in his life, but he refused to let them defeat him. Instead, he used each setback as an opportunity to grow and learn. His example teaches us that no matter what life throws at us, we can always find a way to rise above it.

Finally, Megicho's story is a reminder of the power of the human spirit. Despite all the challenges he faced, he never lost his faith in life. He never gave up on himself or on the world around him. His story shows us that no matter how difficult things may seem, we always have the power to make a difference in our own lives and in the lives of others.

In conclusion, Megicho's story is a powerful example of what can be achieved when we refuse to give up. His life journey teaches us that it's never too late to turn our lives around and that resilience, faith, and hard work can overcome even the most difficult challenges. His story is an inspiration to all of us.

His Majesty of Prevention: The Condom King of Kenya

The Condom King of Kenya is a fascinating story about one man's quest to promote safe sex and reduce the spread of sexually transmitted diseases (STDs) in his country. The story is unique because it challenges cultural taboos around sex and sexual health in a conservative society. In this paper, we will explore the themes and lessons from the story and expand on their relevance beyond the context of Kenya and even beyond the year 2021, when the story was first shared on social media.

One of the main themes of the story is the importance of education and awareness around STDs and safe sex practices. The Condom King, whose real name is Stanley Ngara, recognized that many people in Kenya did not know what HIV was or how it was transmitted. He saw the need to break the taboo around sex and speak openly about STDs, contraceptives, and safe sex practices. His approach was simple but effective: he dressed up in a king's costume, went around the streets giving out condoms, and explained to people how they worked and why they should be used.

Ngara's approach is significant because it challenges the traditional methods of promoting safe sex. In many parts of the world, sex education is still a taboo subject, and many people are ashamed to talk about it openly. Governments and NGOs have tried various methods to promote safe sex, including distributing condoms and other contraceptives, but these efforts are often met with resistance from conservative communities. Ngara's approach, however, was different. By dressing up in a king's costume, he made himself approachable and non-threatening, and people were more likely to listen to him.

Another theme of the story is the importance of grassroots movements in promoting social change. The Condom King's approach was not a top-down initiative from the government or an international organization. It was a grassroots movement that started with one man's passion to make a difference. Ngara started his campaign in his local community, and it grew from there. Today, he has given out tens of thousands of condoms, and his message has spread far beyond his hometown. His dream is to visit all 54 countries in Africa and train a "king of condoms" in each one.

The Condom King's story is also relevant because it shows the impact that one person can have on a community. Ngara's efforts have saved countless lives, and his message has reached millions of people. His approach to promoting safe sex has been replicated in other parts of the world, and his story has inspired many people to take action in their own communities. The lesson here is that even one person can make a difference, and that we all have the power to create positive change in the world.

The Condom King's story also highlights the importance of breaking down stigmas and stereotypes around sex and sexual health. In many parts of the world, condoms are still associated with promiscuity or immorality. This stigma makes it difficult for people to talk openly about sex and sexual health, and it discourages many people from using condoms or seeking treatment for STDs. The Condom King's approach challenges this stigma by showing that safe sex is for everyone, regardless of their gender, sexual orientation, or social status.

The story also has implications for public health policy. In many countries, including Kenya, there is still a lot of stigma around HIV and other STDs. This stigma makes it difficult for governments and NGOs to promote safe sex practices and distribute condoms and other contraceptives. The Condom King's story shows that grassroots movements can be effective in promoting social change, even in the face of cultural taboos and government resistance. The lesson here is that governments and NGOs should work with local communities and grassroots organizations to promote safe sex practices and reduce the spread of STDs.

In conclusion, the story of the "Condom King of Kenya" is a powerful example of how an individual's passion and determination can bring about positive change in society. Stanley Ngara's personal experience with the devastating effects of HIV/AIDS led him to break the taboo around sex and condoms in Kenya and become an advocate for safe sex practices. Through his unique approach of dressing up as a king and giving out condoms on the streets, Ngara has managed to distribute tens of thousands of condoms every month and educate people about the importance of protecting themselves from sexually transmitted diseases.

Zero-Sum Living: The Hilarious Tale of a Man Who Never Spends a Dime

The video describes the story of a man named Daniel from Singapore who is referred to as a "freegan" because he gets everything for free. He has engineered his life to be as frugal as possible, and he doesn't spend any money. Daniel collects whatever people leave unsold in supermarkets and takes the food that is about to expire, which is perfectly good to eat but not good enough to buy. He even goes dumpster diving at night with his friends to find the most incredible things that people throw away.

Although he has a savings of $150,000, Daniel lives this kind of lifestyle because he doesn't want to contribute to food waste. By sharing food, he has become closer to his neighbours and even made friends with them. He and his friends pick up trash and share 90% of it with those in need. This kind of lifestyle might disgust or shock some people, but what they should really be shocked about is the perfectly good stuff that's being thrown away every day in the garbage.

Food waste is a significant problem worldwide. According to the United Nations Food and Agriculture Organization (FAO), one-third of all food produced worldwide is lost or wasted. That's a staggering 1.3 billion tons of food that goes to waste every year. In developed countries, food waste occurs mostly at the consumer and retail levels, while in developing countries, it occurs mainly at the production and post-harvest levels.

The consequences of food waste are dire. It not only wastes valuable resources like land, water, and energy but also contributes to greenhouse gas emissions, which contribute to climate change. Food waste also has economic and social costs. It reduces the availability of food, drives up food prices, and exacerbates food insecurity, hunger, and poverty.

Reducing food waste is not only an ethical and environmental imperative, but it's also an economic opportunity. The FAO estimates that reducing food waste by just 25% could feed all the world's hungry. Moreover, it could generate significant economic benefits, including cost savings, job creation, and increased resource efficiency.

There are several ways to reduce food waste, such as reducing overproduction, improving supply chain management, promoting better food storage and preservation, and encouraging consumers to make more informed choices about their food consumption. Many countries and organizations have launched campaigns and initiatives to tackle food waste, such as the Save Food Global Initiative, the Zero Hunger Challenge, and the Food Recovery Network.

Individual actions, like those of Daniel and his friends, can also make a difference. By reducing their own food waste and sharing surplus food with others, they are contributing to a more sustainable and equitable food system. They are also raising awareness about the issue of food waste and inspiring others to take action.

In conclusion, the story of Daniel from Singapore highlights the issue of food waste and the role of individuals in reducing it. Food waste is a significant problem worldwide, and it has economic, environmental, and social costs. Reducing food waste is not only an ethical imperative but also an economic opportunity. We can all make a difference by taking individual actions to reduce our own food waste and promoting more sustainable and equitable food systems.

Glitz, Glam, and Guffaws: The Hidden Story of a Beauty Queen

Catriona Gray, a young woman from the Philippines, has achieved worldwide recognition for winning the Miss Universe pageant in 2018. Her journey from struggling financially to becoming a beauty queen and advocate for various causes has been an inspiring one, and it holds valuable lessons for everyone.

Catriona's childhood was marked by frequent moves due to her father's job, which made it difficult for her to make friends and feel settled. However, her parents encouraged her to explore different interests and passions, such as karate, music, singing, and dancing. This upbringing instilled in her a love of diverse experiences and a desire to try new things.

As she grew older, Catriona struggled with financial instability and the pressure of being the breadwinner for her family at a young age. She turned to volunteering, which helped her realize the many things she had to be grateful for and shifted her focus from her own struggles to helping others. Through volunteering, she found her purpose: to become a voice for the poor and underprivileged.

It was through a friend's suggestion that Catriona entered the Miss Universe pageant. She saw this as an opportunity to use the platform of pageantry to advocate for causes she believed in. However, her first attempt at the pageant was a failure, and she returned home with a sense of loss and disappointment.

But Catriona didn't give up. She applied again and this time, she won the Miss Universe title. As a beauty queen, she raised thousands of dollars for the youth in Tondo, Manila, advocated for women's rights and education worldwide, and became a voice for the LGBTQ community.

Today, Catriona has launched her own academy where she teaches others how to be confident, find their voice, take risks, and become their own kind of "queen." Her story highlights the importance of finding purpose in life, rather than just pursuing passions or interests. When we have a sense of purpose, everything else falls into place.

There are several key lessons we can learn from Catriona's story:

- Explore your interests and passions: Catriona's parents encouraged her to try different things, and this allowed her to develop a love for diverse experiences. By exploring our interests and passions, we can gain a better understanding of what truly excites us and what we want to pursue in life.

- Help others: When we are struggling with our own problems, it can be easy to become consumed by them. However, as Catriona discovered, helping others can shift our focus and bring a sense of purpose to our lives.

- Failure is not the end: Catriona's first attempt at the Miss Universe pageant was a failure, but she didn't give up. Instead, she applied again and ultimately achieved her goal. Failure is a natural part of life, and it's important to remember that it doesn't define us or our future success.

- Have a sense of purpose: Catriona found her purpose in advocating for causes she believed in, and this gave her a sense of direction and meaning in life. When we have a clear sense of purpose, it can guide our decisions and actions, and help us stay focused on what truly matters.

- Confidence is key: Catriona's academy focuses on teaching others how to be confident, and this is a crucial skill for success in any area of life. When we believe in ourselves and our abilities, we are more likely to take risks, pursue our goals, and achieve our dreams.

Overall, Catriona Gray's story is an inspiring one that demonstrates the power of finding purpose in life, helping others, and never giving up on our dreams. By applying these lessons to our own lives, we can all strive to become the best versions of ourselves and make a positive impact on the world around us.

Pepperlicious: A World of Heat and Flavours

Ed Currie is the creator of the spiciest pepper in the world. The Carolina Reaper, as it is known, was not naturally occurring but was rather created by Ed through crossbreeding different types of peppers to create a new hybrid pepper that would be even spicier than any other. The Carolina Reaper has been rated by Guinness World Records as the spiciest pepper in the world. Ed's journey towards creating this pepper and his subsequent success is an inspiring story of how passion and perseverance can lead to great things.

Ed's journey began when he was addicted to alcohol. He tried to quit several times but always found himself going back to it. It was only when he discovered that eating spicy peppers helped him forget about his cravings for alcohol that he was finally able to quit drinking for good. Ed became fascinated with growing peppers and started experimenting with different types of pepper plants to see how he could make them even hotter.

Ed's passion for growing peppers became so intense that he started growing them in his neighbours' backyards as well. Eventually, his wife suggested that he start a hot sauce business. Ed took this advice and founded the Puckerbutt Pepper Company, which specializes in making all-natural hot sauces that are some of the spiciest in the world. The Puckerbutt Pepper Company's sauces are made without any chemicals or additives, which makes them a healthier choice for people who love spicy food.

Ed's hot sauces were so popular that one of his peppers, the Carolina Reaper, broke the Guinness World Record for being the spiciest pepper in the world. The Carolina Reaper has a Scoville rating of over 2 million, which means that it is over 400 times hotter than a jalapeño pepper. The heat of the Carolina Reaper is so intense that it can literally make you cry, and it is not recommended for people who are not used to eating spicy food.

Ed's success with his hot sauce business did not stop at making him rich. His peppers have also been used for research purposes. Capsaicin, the chemical compound found in peppers that gives them their spiciness, has health benefits such as aiding digestion and affecting cancer cells. Ed's peppers are being used by scientists to help children with obesity and contribute to cancer research. The Puckerbutt Pepper Company is also working on creating even hotter peppers, not to break any records, but to help people who are suffering from various health issues.

Ed's story is an inspiring one, as it shows that a passion for something can lead to great things. He was able to turn his addiction into a positive outcome by creating something that not only helped him but also helped others. His success also shows that taking risks and pursuing one's dreams can lead to great rewards. Ed's hot sauce business is a testament to the fact that sometimes the simplest things in life, like a hot pepper, can make a big difference.

In conclusion, Ed Currie's story of creating the spiciest pepper in the world is an inspiring one. It shows that passion, perseverance, and taking risks can lead to great things. His journey from being addicted to alcohol to becoming a successful entrepreneur is a story that should inspire everyone to follow their dreams and never give up. Furthermore, the health benefits associated with capsaicin, the chemical compound found in peppers, are a reminder that sometimes the simplest things in life can have a significant impact on our health and well-being.

The Human Tornado: Meet the Man Who Speaks Faster Than Eminem

Humans have a wide range of talents and abilities, and some people possess extraordinary skills that set them apart from others. John is one such individual who has an exceptional talent for speaking fast. He has honed this talent over the years, making it his profession, and even earning recognition in the Guinness World Records.

John's story highlights the importance of discovering one's unique abilities and pursuing them passionately. He discovered his talent for speaking fast when he was only 12 years old, and he continued to practice and refine his skill every day. This dedication to his craft eventually helped him make a living out of it, appearing in TV shows, movies, and commercials. His success shows that it is possible to turn one's unique abilities into a career and make a living doing what one loves.

John's story also illustrates the importance of where and how one grows up, as his upbringing in New York, with three sisters, and his Italian heritage all played a role in shaping his unique talent. Growing up in New York, he believes that people tend to talk faster, and being from an Italian family made him naturally animated and talk quickly. These factors, combined with his love for Shakespeare, helped him develop his fast-speaking ability.

Moreover, John's story highlights the value of perseverance and the need to keep practicing one's craft. Even after achieving his goal of winning the charity fair, John did not stop practicing. Instead, he continued to refine his skill, and this helped him improve his craft over time.

John's success also shows that there are numerous ways to pursue one's passion, and there is no one-size-fits-all approach. He found a unique way to monetize his skill, and it worked out for him. His experience illustrates the importance of finding a career that aligns with one's interests and skills and provides a sense of fulfilment.

Furthermore, John's story underscores the need to find a purpose in life, and this involves discovering what one loves and finding a way to pursue it. For John, talking fast is not just a skill, but a passion that has become an integral part of his life. He believes that the secret to life is figuring out what one loves to do and finding a way to make a living doing it.

In conclusion, John's story serves as an inspiration to people worldwide to discover and pursue their unique talents and passions. His experience highlights the value of hard work, perseverance, and dedication to honing one's skills. It also underscores the importance of finding a career that aligns with one's interests and skills and provides a sense of purpose and fulfilment. John's story is a reminder that everyone has a unique talent, and with the right mindset and effort, it is possible to turn that talent into a successful career.

The Art of Recycling: When Old Jeans Become New Paintings

Ian Berry, also known as Denimu, is an artist who creates intricate and realistic artwork using denim jeans. Berry's unique approach to art has made him famous worldwide, as he has been featured in various museums, galleries, and exhibitions. Berry's artwork is not only visually stunning but also sends a powerful message about waste and recycling.

Berry's artwork began with an observation that all jeans have a different shade, depending on their age, wear, and wash. Berry realized that he could use these shades to create different colours, just like an artist would use paints. He started collecting old and discarded jeans that people had thrown away, from friends, thrift shops, and even strangers. By gathering thousands of jeans, Berry could use them as a palette to create his artwork.

Berry's art is not only visually stunning but also has an emotional impact on people. He depicts everyday objects and places that people see all the time, such as laundromats, pubs, and streets, but by using denim, he shows them in a new light. By combining denim with realistic art, Berry creates a unique perspective on ordinary life. The jeans give the artwork a textured and rugged look that adds depth and realism to the image.

Berry's technique involves taking a photograph of what he wants to make and then analysing the colour and lighting to choose the right jeans. He then cuts the jeans into small pieces and glues them onto a huge canvas made of denim jeans. Berry's artwork takes an incredible amount of time and effort, with some pieces taking up to six months to complete. He has created many large-scale artworks, which can measure several feet in size.

Berry's artwork has become a popular attraction in various exhibitions worldwide. His work has been featured in shopping malls, museums, and magazines. Berry's unique approach to art has won him many accolades, and he has become an inspiration to many young artists worldwide. Berry's artwork has also caught the attention of many collectors, who have paid thousands of dollars for his pieces.

Berry's artwork is not just about creating stunning pieces of art, but also about sending a powerful message about waste and recycling. His work shows that anything can be transformed into something beautiful if we use our creativity and imagination. Berry's artwork inspires people to think about the waste they generate and how they can use it creatively.

Berry's approach to art is not typical, and it challenges the traditional notions of art. He uses everyday materials to create something extraordinary, and his art is not limited by traditional mediums like paints or pencils. Berry's artwork shows that anything can be transformed into art, and the possibilities are endless.

In conclusion, Ian Berry's approach to art is unique and inspiring. He uses discarded denim jeans to create intricate and realistic artwork that challenges traditional notions of art. His work sends a powerful message about waste and recycling and shows that anything can be transformed into something beautiful. Berry's artwork is not just visually stunning, but it also has an emotional impact on people. His work is a testament to the power of creativity and imagination and shows that the possibilities are endless.

Butt-iful Creations: The Smoking Hot Toy Line

Naman Gupta, an entrepreneur from New Delhi, India, found a way to turn cigarette butts into gold by upcycling them into various new products. Cigarette butts are one of the most common forms of litter found on the streets. According to a study by the International Coastal Clean-up, cigarette butts account for approximately 30% of all litter collected from the world's beaches and waterways. It is estimated that nearly 12 billion cigarette butts are thrown away every day, creating a major environmental problem.

Naman noticed this problem and decided to do something about it. He began collecting cigarette butts from the streets and experimenting with ways to recycle them. Despite having no background in science, he developed an organic formula that can turn cigarette filters into white cotton in just 2.5 days. Naman's innovative idea led to the establishment of a filter recycling factory that recycles cigarette butts into various new products, including pillows, dolls, chairs, jewellery, keychains, and buttons.

Naman's process of recycling cigarette butts is called upcycling instead of recycling because he creates new materials of greater quality. Upcycling is a process of converting waste materials into new products of higher quality or value. It involves finding new uses for discarded materials rather than simply throwing them away. Upcycling helps to reduce waste, conserve natural resources, and reduce the environmental impact of manufacturing.

Upcycling has become an important trend in recent years, with many companies and individuals embracing the concept of turning waste into something valuable. The upcycling movement has led to the creation of many innovative products and designs, ranging from furniture made from recycled materials to clothing made from discarded fabrics.

Naman's company not only helps to reduce waste but also provides employment opportunities for people in his community. He pays people to collect cigarette butts from the streets, creating jobs for many who would otherwise struggle to find work. His business also creates new markets for the products made from upcycled cigarette butts, providing income opportunities for local artisans and entrepreneurs.

The upcycling of cigarette butts also has significant environmental benefits. The recycling of cigarette butts helps to reduce the amount of waste that ends up in landfills, reducing the risk of groundwater contamination and reducing greenhouse gas emissions. Recycling cigarette butts also helps to conserve natural resources, such as water and energy, that are used in the manufacturing of new products.

In addition to the environmental benefits, upcycling cigarette butts also has important social benefits. The recycling of cigarette butts creates jobs and income opportunities for people in the community, providing economic benefits that can help to alleviate poverty and improve livelihoods.

The upcycling movement has gained significant momentum in recent years, with many individuals and companies embracing the concept of turning waste into something valuable. The upcycling of cigarette butts is just one example of how waste can be transformed into something useful and valuable. The success of Naman's business has inspired others to consider upcycling as a way to reduce waste and create new economic opportunities.

In conclusion, Naman Gupta's innovative idea of upcycling cigarette butts into new products has significant environmental, social, and economic benefits. His business not only helps to reduce waste but also provides employment opportunities for people in his community. The upcycling of cigarette butts is just one example of how waste can be transformed into something useful and valuable. As the upcycling movement gains momentum, we can expect to see more innovative ideas that turn waste into valuable products, benefiting both the environment and society.

The Great Eiffel Tower Heist (of Data): How One Group is Preserving History

Cultural heritage refers to the collection of artistic, historical, and scientific accomplishments that define and give meaning to a society's identity. Cultural heritage is, unfortunately, vulnerable to destruction from a variety of causes. Monuments, buildings, and art can be destroyed by natural disasters, war, terrorism, and vandalism. Historical artifacts can be lost due to theft, decay, or neglect. Therefore, the preservation of cultural heritage is vital to humanity, and it is the responsibility of individuals, governments, and organizations to protect and conserve it for future generations.

The preservation of cultural heritage is a complex and challenging task, as it requires balancing the need to protect the heritage while making it accessible to the public. Fortunately, technology has provided several solutions to this issue, and Piql is an excellent example of how technology can be used to preserve cultural heritage.

Piql is a Norwegian company that has created a technology that preserves global cultural heritage for eternity. The founder of Piql, Rune Bjerkestrand, and his team are on a mission to save global cultural heritage by collecting monuments, paintings, and other artifacts from cultures around the world. They scan these artifacts and turn them into data. This data can be used to recreate whatever is lost in the future. For instance, if the Eiffel Tower were to disappear, it could be recreated using the data stored by Piql.

Storing cultural heritage data on computers, servers, or even the cloud is not safe enough, as they can be destroyed or hacked. Therefore, Piql prints the data onto a highly resistant film that can also store human-readable information. This film is so tiny that all the monuments seen in a person's life can be stored on it. The film is incredibly durable, and once printed, it can be stored in the safest location on earth: the Arctic World Archive.

The Arctic World Archive is an underground vault located in the Arctic, which is safe from nuclear attacks. The vault has no light, air conditioning, heating, electricity, or service, making it have the lowest possible carbon footprint. The stored data can last over a thousand years, and in the case of a disaster, the world's culture can be restored easily using a magnifying glass and a phone. The Arctic World Archive is the perfect location for storing the film as the Arctic is naturally cold, dry, dark, and has low oxygen, which is ideal for preserving the film.

Piql has made it possible to store all kinds of data, such as historical artifacts, scientific discoveries, and genetic code. They can receive any kind of data that can be converted to ones and zeros, and they can write it to the pickle film. The technology developed by Piql is a holistic solution that provides secure long-term preservation of cultural heritage. It took them 11 years and 41 million euros to develop this technology.

The preservation of cultural heritage is critical to human history and identity. By preserving cultural heritage, we can learn from the past and build a better future. Technology has made it possible to preserve cultural heritage for future generations. The technology developed by Piql is an excellent example of how technology can be used to preserve cultural heritage.

In conclusion, the preservation of cultural heritage is a critical task that requires a concerted effort from individuals, governments, and organizations. Technology has made it possible to preserve cultural heritage for future generations. Piql is a great example of how technology can be used to preserve cultural heritage. By scanning monuments, paintings, and other artifacts and turning them into data, Piql has created a way to preserve cultural heritage for eternity. The Arctic World Archive, with its ideal preservation conditions, is the perfect location to store the data. Piql has made it possible to preserve all kinds of data, making their technology a holistic solution for the preservation of cultural heritage.

Brick by Brick: The Lego Man's Rise to Superhero Status

David Aguilar, also known as "Hand Solo," is a young man from Spain who was born with a condition called Poland Syndrome. This condition affects the development of the chest muscles, causing them to be underdeveloped or absent. It can also affect other muscles in the body, including those in the arms, back, and abdomen.

As a result of his condition, David's right arm is significantly smaller than his left and has limited function. Growing up, David was often bullied by his peers due to his appearance, and he found it difficult to make friends. However, he found solace in playing with Legos, which allowed him to escape from the outside world and express his creativity.

Over time, David's love of Legos turned into a passion for building, and he began to create more complex structures using the colourful plastic bricks. He started with simple designs and gradually worked his way up to more complicated models, such as cars, robots, and even a functional pinball machine.

Despite the limitations of his right arm, David's love for building never wavered, and he began to experiment with building prosthetic arms using Legos. His first attempt was a crude design that was little more than a plastic extension of his arm, but over time, he refined his techniques and built increasingly sophisticated prosthetic devices.

One of David's most impressive creations is his MK-1 Lego arm, which is a fully functional prosthetic that he built using 700 Lego bricks. The arm can be controlled using his left arm and has a motor, fingers, and even a pressure sensor that allows David to pick up and hold objects with great precision. He has also built other prosthetic devices, including a functioning robotic arm that he controls with a smartphone.

David's creations have garnered attention from around the world, and he has been featured in numerous news outlets and media platforms. He has also been recognized for his work by the Guinness World Records, which awarded him a certificate for creating the world's first functional Lego prosthetic arm.

But David's work is not just about creating cool gadgets and gaining recognition for his achievements. He is passionate about using his skills to help others who, like himself, may not have access to expensive prosthetic devices. In an interview with BBC, he explained that his ultimate goal is to create affordable prosthetics that can be used by people all over the world, regardless of their financial situation.

To this end, David has created a YouTube channel where he shares tutorials and tips for building prosthetic arms using Lego bricks. He also runs a charity organization called Hand Solo that aims to provide affordable prosthetics to people who need them.

David's story is a testament to the power of creativity and perseverance in the face of adversity. Despite the challenges posed by his condition, he has found a way to pursue his passion for building and use his skills to help others. His work has inspired countless people around the world and serves as a reminder that anyone can make a difference, regardless of their circumstances.

In conclusion, David Aguilar is a real-life Tony Stark who has used his passion for building to create functional prosthetic arms using Lego bricks. His story is an inspiration to anyone who has faced adversity and found a way to overcome it through creativity and perseverance. David's work is a testament to the power of innovation and the importance of using our skills to help others. His creations are not just cool gadgets; they are life-changing devices that have the potential to improve the lives of people all over the world.

Gravity's Worst Nightmare: The Balancing Act of Rocky

The story of Rocky, the balancing artist, is one of inspiration and perseverance. At a time when he was at his lowest point in life, his marriage had ended and he felt like a failure, he found happiness in the most unlikely place - balancing stones. Rocky discovered that he had a talent for balancing objects, and he began with stones, eventually moving on to bigger objects like bikes, machines, and even people. He has been doing this every day for the past 13 years.

What makes Rocky's story so compelling is his determination to find joy in his life again. When he was feeling down, he tried different things to keep himself busy, like traveling and adventure sports, but nothing helped. However, the moment he discovered his talent for balancing stones, he found something that he truly loved, something that made him happy.

Rocky's talent is not magic, but rather science. To balance an object, you need to find its centre and understand gravity. Rocky has mastered these concepts, and he can balance anything that he sets his mind to. His creations are not just structures; they are works of art that showcase his talent and creativity.

One of the most important lessons that Rocky teaches us is the importance of finding something that you truly love. When you do something that you enjoy, it doesn't feel like work. Instead, it feels like you are living your life to the fullest. Rocky is not doing this for the money or the fame; he is doing it because it makes him happy.

Rocky's story is a reminder that everyone has talents and passions that they can pursue. Sometimes, it takes a difficult situation to help us discover these things, but when we do, it can bring us immense joy and fulfilment. We should all take the time to explore our interests and discover what makes us happy.

Moreover, Rocky's story also highlights the importance of practice and determination. He has been practicing his art every day for the past 13 years, and he never stops challenging himself. Through his perseverance, he has become one of the most famous balancing artists in Korea, and he has even travelled around the world to showcase his talent.

In conclusion, Rocky's story is an inspiring tale of how one person can turn their life around by finding something that they love. Through his talent for balancing objects, Rocky has become a true artist, creating stunning structures that showcase his creativity and mastery of science. His story reminds us that everyone has talents and passions that they can pursue, and that finding joy in our lives is essential to our well-being.

Waiting Pays Off: The Lucrative World of Line Sitting

The concept of waiting in line has been around for centuries, as people have always had to wait for something they want or need. From standing in line for tickets to a concert or waiting in line for a new iPhone release, the act of waiting in line can be time-consuming, boring, and often frustrating. However, one man has turned this concept of waiting in line into a lucrative business.

Robert Samuel, the founder of Same Ole Line Dudes, started his business out of necessity. He was unemployed and needed money, and he saw a unique opportunity when he saw wealthy people waiting in line for hours outside an Apple store to purchase the newest iPhone. Samuel offered to stand in line for one person for $350, and the rest is history. Since then, Same Ole Line Dudes has become a thriving business, offering line-sitting services for various items and services.

The success of Same Ole Line Dudes is a testament to the fact that there is a demand for people who are willing to wait in line for others. This business model has proven to be successful not only in New York but also in other parts of the world. In places like Singapore and Hong Kong, companies have been offering similar services for years, catering to people who don't have the time or patience to wait in line themselves.

The idea of waiting in line for someone else is not new, but the way Same Ole Line Dudes has approached it is innovative. The company has a slogan, "We wait for your one," which means they will wait in line for anything that a customer wants, from the latest iPhone to government applications. They advertise their services by giving out business cards to people in line, using a banner on the sidewalk, and even doing chalk advertisements. The company has also received a lot of attention from the media, which has helped to promote their business.

The success of Same Ole Line Dudes has also shown that there is a market for people who are willing to pay for convenience. People are willing to pay a premium to have someone else wait in line for them, saving them time and hassle. This idea has been around for years, with companies like Uber and Grubhub catering to people who want convenience and are willing to pay for it. Same Ole Line Dudes has tapped into this market and created a business that is both profitable and sustainable.

The growth of Same Ole Line Dudes has also led to job creation. The company has hired people from all walks of life, from stay-at-home moms to college students to seniors and veterans. The job of a line sitter is not physically demanding, which means that people of all ages and abilities can do it. This has provided job opportunities for people who may not be able to work traditional jobs or who are looking for a side hustle to earn extra income.

In conclusion, Same Ole Line Dudes has shown that there is a market for people who are willing to pay for convenience. The success of this business has also demonstrated that there are opportunities to create businesses out of seemingly mundane tasks like waiting in line. The concept of waiting in line for others may seem odd, but it has proven to be a profitable and sustainable business model. As technology continues to evolve and people's lives become busier, it's likely that businesses like Same Ole Line Dudes will continue to thrive.

Paws Behind Bars: Why Dogs Are Doing Hard Time

Dogs are widely considered to be man's best friend. They are loyal, loving, and provide companionship to their owners. However, in some cases, dogs can hurt or kill people or other animals, and this can lead to them being put on death row in some states in the USA. This is where the dog lawyer, Richard Rosenthal, comes in.

Richard is a lawyer who specializes in defending dogs who are on death row. He has helped save over 200 dogs through his non-profit organization, The Lexus Project. His work involves going to court to defend dogs who are accused of hurting or killing people or animals. Richard believes that dogs should have a voice and that it's his job to defend them when they cannot defend themselves.

The justice system in the USA requires dogs to go to court if they hurt or kill someone or another animal. The dog is then put on trial like a real criminal, and if it loses the case, it may be sentenced to death row. This can be a traumatic experience for both the dog and its owner, who may be emotionally attached to the dog. This is why Richard's work is so important, as he provides a voice for the dogs and works tirelessly to save them from being put down.

There is a lot of debate on whether dogs should be put down if they hurt or kill someone or another animal. Some people believe that it's not fair to kill dogs as it's not always their fault and they cannot defend themselves. Others believe that dogs should be put down as they pose a danger to society. Richard's work has highlighted this debate, and he has faced a lot of criticism from people who disagree with his views.

Despite the criticism, Richard continues to fight for the rights of dogs. He has even received death threats for what he does, but he remains undeterred. Richard's work has helped to change the way that dogs are treated in the justice system. He has helped to give dogs a voice and has saved many of them from being put to death.

Richard's work is not only important for dogs but for all animals who cannot defend themselves. He believes that the justice system should work for those who don't have a voice, not against them. His work has shown that even animals should be treated with respect and dignity and that they deserve to be defended when they cannot defend themselves.

In conclusion, the work of the dog lawyer, Richard Rosenthal, is an example of how individuals can make a difference in the lives of others. His work has helped to change the way that dogs are treated in the justice system, and he has saved the lives of many dogs through his non-profit organization, The Lexus Project. His work is not only important for dogs but for all animals who cannot defend themselves. Richard's courage and determination to fight for what he believes in is an inspiration to us all, and his work has shown that even the smallest voices deserve to be heard.

Talking to the Animals: Jane Goodall's Wild Adventures

Dr. Jane Goodall is a renowned primatologist and conservationist who has spent over 60 years studying chimpanzees and other primates. She has made significant contributions to the scientific community, including the discovery that chimpanzees have their own complex social structures and can use tools to accomplish tasks.

Dr. Goodall's research has also shed light on the close genetic relationship between humans and chimpanzees. Humans share approximately 98.7% of their DNA with chimpanzees, making them our closest living relatives. This finding has important implications for our understanding of evolution and the origins of human behavior.

In addition to her scientific contributions, Dr. Goodall has also become a prominent environmental and animal rights activist. She founded the Jane Goodall Institute in 1977, which works to protect chimpanzees and their habitats through research, education, and conservation efforts. The institute has also expanded its mission to include community development programs and youth education initiatives.

One of the most significant threats to chimpanzees and other primates is habitat destruction. Deforestation, mining, and other human activities have led to the loss of crucial forest habitats for many primate species. This has a devastating impact on these animals, as they depend on the forest for food, shelter, and social interaction. The Jane Goodall Institute works to protect chimpanzee habitats by partnering with local communities to promote sustainable agriculture, ecotourism, and other conservation efforts.

Another major threat to chimpanzees is the illegal wildlife trade. Chimpanzees are often captured and sold as pets or used in medical research, which can have severe consequences for their welfare and survival. The Jane Goodall Institute works to combat the illegal wildlife trade by supporting law enforcement efforts and promoting public awareness about the importance of protecting primates and other wildlife.

Dr. Goodall has also been a vocal advocate for animal rights and welfare. She has spoken out against animal testing and the use of animals for entertainment, and has been a strong proponent of veganism and vegetarianism. Her work has helped to raise public awareness about the ethical considerations surrounding the use of animals for human purposes.

In addition to her conservation and advocacy work, Dr. Goodall has also been a champion of youth education and empowerment. She founded the Roots & Shoots program in 1991, which is a global youth-led initiative that promotes environmental and community service projects. The program has engaged thousands of young people around the world in efforts to make a positive impact on their communities and the planet.

Overall, Dr. Goodall's contributions to the scientific community and the world of conservation and animal rights have been significant and far-reaching. Her work has helped to deepen our understanding of the natural world and our place in it, and has inspired countless individuals to take action to protect our planet and its inhabitants.

The Fish are Back and the Birds are Singing: A Miracle Cure for a Contaminated Lake

The issue of pollution in our lakes and rivers is a problem that affects the entire world. Contaminated water sources cause problems for both humans and wildlife, and it is a difficult problem to solve. However, one man, Marino, has found a unique solution that has transformed a polluted lake into a clean one.

Marino's childhood lake was contaminated, and he decided to do something about it. He came up with a solution that attracts contaminated particles and floats them to the top. The solution is 100% organic, and it is safe to consume. Marino treated the contaminated lake with biofilters, nanotechnology, and biology to transform it into a clean, safe lake for humans and wildlife.

Marino's solution is expensive and difficult to implement, but it is not impossible. He was able to get a loan and dedicate his time to solving this problem. Marino's solution is an excellent example of how one person can make a significant impact on the environment. We need more people like Marino to help solve the world's environmental problems.

Polluted lakes and rivers are a significant problem around the world. According to data, 40% of the world's lakes and rivers are contaminated. The contamination of water sources is a problem that affects both humans and wildlife. Polluted water can cause health problems for humans, and it can also harm wildlife by killing off fish and other aquatic life.

Marino's solution to cleaning the lake is unique because it is organic and environmentally friendly. The solution he created attracts the contaminated particles and floats them to the top. This process makes it easy to remove the pollution from the water.

Marino's solution is not just a quick fix; he treated the contaminated lake with biofilters, nanotechnology, and biology. This process took several months, but it resulted in a complete transformation of the lake. The lake went from being polluted and unsafe to clean and safe for humans and wildlife.

Marino's solution is expensive and difficult to implement. He was able to get a loan and dedicate his time to solving this problem, but not everyone has the resources to do so. The cost of implementing Marino's solution may be prohibitive for some communities.

Marino's solution is an excellent example of how one person can make a significant impact on the environment. We need more people like Marino to help solve the world's environmental problems. It is not enough to rely on governments and large organizations to solve these problems. We need individuals who are willing to take the initiative and find solutions to environmental problems.

Marino's solution to cleaning the lake is just the beginning. We need more solutions like this to solve the world's environmental problems. We need to find ways to reduce pollution and protect our lakes and rivers. This problem affects everyone, and we all have a role to play in finding solutions.

One way we can reduce pollution is by using fewer chemicals in our daily lives. We should also be mindful of what we put down our drains and what we throw away. We need to find ways to recycle more and reduce our waste. Small changes can make a big difference in reducing pollution.

Governments and organizations can also help by providing funding for environmental solutions. We need more research and development into environmentally friendly solutions. We also need regulations that protect our lakes and rivers from pollution.

In conclusion, Marino's solution to cleaning a polluted lake is an excellent example of how one person can make a significant impact on the environment. We need more solutions like this to solve the world's environmental problems. We all have a role to play in finding solutions to environmental problems. Governments, organizations, and individuals can work together to find ways to reduce pollution and protect our lakes and rivers. By taking small steps, we can make a big difference in reducing pollution and protecting the environment.

Did you love *60 Miracles of Humanity*? Then you should read *Life Illumination: 100 TEDx Talks to treasure*[1] by Rohan Aggarwal!

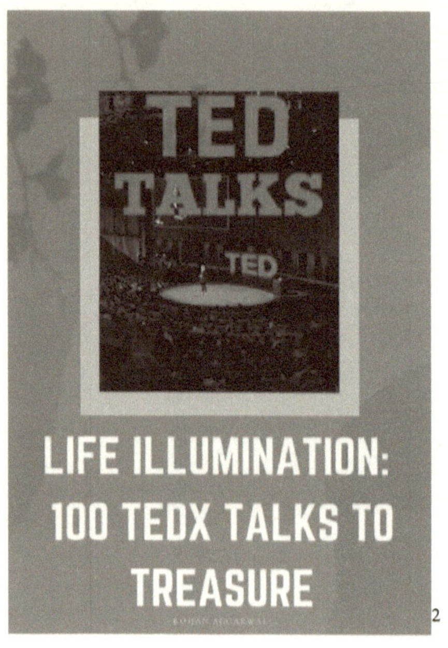

"Unlock the power of innovative ideas and groundbreaking insights with this comprehensive collection of 100 TEDx Talks. This book brings together the most inspiring voices of our time to share their stories, passions, and vision for a better world. Whether you're seeking inspiration for your own life or looking to spark a revolution, this book is the ultimate source of wisdom, creativity, and inspiration.

"Dive into a diverse array of topics, from science and technology to art and social change, and be captivated by the unique and powerful perspectives of the world's most innovative thinkers. Each talk has been carefully curated for its impact and relevance, providing a

---

1. https://books2read.com/u/bwyyaG

2. https://books2read.com/u/bwyyaG

thought-provoking and empowering perspective on the world we live in.

With "Life Illumination: 100 TEDx Talks to treasure", you'll gain access to a wealth of knowledge and unlock the potential for positive change. Whether you're looking to improve your relationships, achieve your goals, or simply find more joy and fulfillment in life, this book offers practical, actionable advice for developing a positive mindset and overcoming the obstacles that hold you back.

"So, sit back, get ready to be inspired, and let the ideas of the world's most visionary thinkers change your life forever. Order your copy of "Life Illumination: 100 TEDx Talks to treasure" today and discover the power of great ideas!"

About the Author

Introducing a top-selling author who has captured the hearts and minds of readers worldwide with their captivating storytelling and insightful perspectives. With two books under their belt, this author has established themselves as a master of their craft, captivating readers with their unique blend of humor, pathos, and heart. Their writing is characterized by a deep understanding of the human condition, exploring the complexities of relationships, the challenges of modern life, and the power of the human spirit. Whether you're a fan of fiction or non-fiction, this author has something to offer, with a diverse range of topics that are sure to captivate and inspire. So why wait? Discover the captivating world of this top-selling author today and see for yourself why they have become a literary sensation!